# what do we know and what should we do about...?

Sara Miller McCune founded SAGE Publishing in 1965 to support the dissemination of usable knowledge and educate a global community. SAGE publishes more than 1000 journals and over 800 new books each year, spanning a wide range of subject areas. Our growing selection of library products includes archives, data, case studies and video. SAGE remains majority owned by our founder and after her lifetime will become owned by a charitable trust that secures the company's continued independence.

Los Angeles | London | New Delhi | Singapore | Washington DC | Melbourne

# what do we know and what should we do about...?

# AI

Ewa Luger

Los Angeles | London | New Delhi
Singapore | Washington DC | Melbourne

Los Angeles | London | New Delhi
Singapore | Washington DC | Melbourne

SAGE Publications Ltd
1 Oliver's Yard
55 City Road
London EC1Y 1SP

SAGE Publications Inc.
2455 Teller Road
Thousand Oaks, California 91320

SAGE Publications India Pvt Ltd
B 1/I 1 Mohan Cooperative Industrial
Area
Mathura Road
New Delhi 110 044

SAGE Publications Asia-Pacific Pte Ltd
3 Church Street
#10-04 Samsung Hub
Singapore 049483

Editor: Natalie Aguilera
Assistant editor: Rhoda Ola-Said
Production editor: Sarah Sewell
Copyeditor: Catja Pafort
Indexer: Charmian Parkin
Marketing manager: Ruslana Khatagova
Cover design: Wendy Scott
Typeset by: C&M Digitals (P) Ltd, Chennai, India
Printed in the UK

**Library of Congress Control Number:
2022942884**

**British Library Cataloguing in Publication data**

A catalogue record for this book is available from
the British Library

ISBN 978-1-5296-0028-5
ISBN 978-1-5296-0027-8 (pbk)

At SAGE we take sustainability seriously. Most of our products are printed in the UK using
responsibly sourced papers and boards. When we print overseas we ensure sustainable papers are
used as measured by the PREPS grading system. We undertake an annual audit to monitor our
sustainability.

# contents

# titles in the series

# about the series

Every news bulletin carries stories which relate in some way to the social sciences – most obviously politics, economics and sociology, but also, often, anthropology, business studies, security studies, criminology, geography and many others.

Yet despite the existence of large numbers of academics who research these subjects, relatively little of their work is known to the general public.

There are many reasons for that, but, arguably, it is that the kinds of formats that social scientists publish in, and the way in which they write, are simply not accessible to the general public.

The guiding theme of this series is to provide a format and a way of writing which addresses this problem. Each book in the series is concerned with a topic of widespread public interest, and each is written in a way which is readily understandable to the general reader with no particular background knowledge.

The authors are academics with an established reputation and a track record of research in the relevant subject. They provide an overview of the research knowledge about the subject, whether this be long-established or reporting the most recent findings, widely accepted or still controversial. Often in public debate there is a demand for greater clarity about the facts, and that is one of the things the books in this series provide.

However, in social sciences, facts are often disputed and subject to different interpretations. They do not always, or even often, 'speak for themselves'. The authors therefore strive to show the different interpretations or the key controversies about their topics, but without getting bogged down in arcane academic arguments.

Not only can there be disputes about facts but also there are almost invariably different views on what should follow from these facts. And, in any case, public debate requires more of academics than just to report facts; it is also necessary to make suggestions and recommendations about the implications of these facts.

Thus each volume also contains ideas about 'what we should do' within each topic area. These are based upon the authors' knowledge of the field but also, inevitably, upon their own views, values and preferences. Readers may not agree with them, but the intention is to provoke thought and well-informed debate.

Chris Grey, Series Editor

Professor of Organization Studies

Royal Holloway, University of London

# about the author

**Ewa Luger** is Professor of Human-Data Interaction at the University of Edinburgh, Co-Director of the Institute of Design Informatics, Fellow of the Alan Turing Institute, and Director of Research Innovation for Edinburgh College of Art. Her research explores the social, ethical and design implications of Artificial Intelligence. She advises government and industry and was previously a researcher at Microsoft Research and a fellow at Corpus Christi College, University of Cambridge.

# introduction

In 1999, prior to becoming an academic, I worked for a UK charity. I had previously used neither a personal email address nor regularly used a computer and, having been raised by an immigrant family who suffered the vagaries of an unstable political climate, I was highly privacy-conscious and wary of authority. This was no doubt the influence of my grandmother who would describe memories of monitored calls and the tales of what happened when people said the wrong thing in the wrong place. Fast forward 22 years and I merrily chat away to my voice assistant, google my personal health symptoms, and make openly political comments in public forums. Whilst some of this is attributable to my experience of nothing bad resulting, a large part is the product of the nature of the systems with which I interact. My voice assistant makes my life a little bit easier when I want to listen to something hands-free, Google at my fingertips means that I can find information on pretty much everything, and the short-form nature of most social media platforms enables the publication of anything that pops into mind. If asked, I would probably say that I am a highly private person, but just a quick view of my online activities suggests that what I understand by private is quite different from prior generations of my family. Or perhaps, because the activities I describe occur mostly within the confines of my home or through one of my personal devices, one could argue that I might reasonably expect a level of privacy. Either way, I knowingly use each system and, because my time is tight and they are designed to be unobtrusive when used, I gloss over the implications and cede control to the devices in my life.

What I don't see, of course, are the complex processes that underpin those device interactions (how my data are processed), who gets to see them (how my data are shared), how the decisions about the content I see are being made (how the underpinning algorithms work), or who ultimately controls things in each case (who owns or finances the platforms). Each of the systems I have described are made functional through the algorithms they employ and each relies on huge amounts of training data so that they can better enable services and user experience. But this is not all they do. Harvard professor Shoshana Zuboff claims that this model of data-monetisation underpinning our online services is just the latest form of economic exploitation. In her 2019 book, *The Age of Surveillance Capitalism*, she explains that everyday human experience has been transformed into behavioural capital. Whilst some of the data collected about us online are important for service improvement, an increasing amount of data are simply collected because companies can, creating a source of proprietary behavioural surplus, owned by corporations, and used to improve machine intelligence. Zuboff calls these Machine Learning (ML) outcomes Prediction Products, which function to anticipate what we as humans might do in the future, and on this basis create futures markets within which trading occurs, essentially making us unpaid and unknowing producers of free raw materials. Whether or not this argument rings true, it is evident that all of these systems are owned by large multinationals who arguably have more control over our behaviour, and insight into our lives, than many nation states.

It has been claimed that, if all the algorithms in the world stopped working, life as we know it would cease to exist (Domingos, 2015). We have also been told by reliable sources that AI will replace the majority of jobs and, if we wait long enough, such systems will become sufficiently self-aware to take over the world. Whilst this last claim is more science fiction than fact, we are, in reality, already pretty dependant on algorithms in our everyday lives and technology has indeed massively impacted the workplace. Despite such developments, much of the hyperbole, though probably stimulated by research somewhere, should rarely be taken at face value. Artificial General Intelligence (AGI), the notion of AI indistinguishable from human intelligence, is still theoretical, and whilst no one has substantially challenged the idea that AI might eventually mimic or match humans on most tasks (Tegmark, 2017: 92), this is not happening anytime soon. So, we can relax, set the idea of AGI aside and focus on where we are with developments right now. Similarly, the idea of robots also tends to push us towards particular visions of the future. Originally a sub-field of mechanical engineering, it is useful to note that recent robot capability is a direct result of 'AI-based control structures' (Franklin, 2014: 27) enabling more complex tasks such as walking upstairs or dancing. Robotics is therefore related to AI, but a separate field that focuses on embodiment, and creating agents that perform tasks without human intervention. Whilst there is clearly a relationship, the challenges are quite different and so I will not be covering robotics in any depth but if, at this point, you would like to see some really sophisticated robots in action, then type Boston Dynamics into a search engine and enjoy. It was in fact these cute little robotic chaps that inspired Charlie Brooker's Black Mirror episode *Metalhead*, which featured the kind of unrelenting human-hunting dog-shaped robots that are the stuff of nightmares (Hibberd, 2017).

Setting dancing robots aside, the best way to really navigate the complexity of AI myths and half-truths is to gain a little understanding of the basics of the core subject matter. So, while we are not likely to be overtaken by killer bots tomorrow, it is probably still a good idea to understand the basics of what we're dealing with when we talk about AI. To start that journey, this introduction will take you on a whistle-stop tour of some of the common concepts and approaches you may have heard mentioned in the same breath as the term Artificial Intelligence (AI). Many of these ideas will be complex, nuanced and require specialised understanding. However, my job here is to reduce these concepts down into the basics of what is meant when you hear these terms in use.

# So, what exactly is Artificial Intelligence?

The term 'artificial intelligence', or AI, represents a sphere of research and development within the discipline of Computer Science that is character-ised by specific trends and controversies (Franklin, 2014). In this way AI is not really one thing, but describes a constellation of methods, approaches and technologies that help systems mimic aspects of natural intelligence. Originating in the middle of the last century, AI is both diverse and con-stantly evolving and, as such, has so far evaded a consistent and agreed upon definition amongst AI scholars.

Essentially, when we use the term, we are describing the capacity of a computational system, be that a digital computer or a robot, to perform the particular tasks one might commonly expect of a human or other intelligent being. More formally, it is an 'approach to understanding, modelling, and replicating intelligence and cognitive processes by invoking various compu-tational, mathematical, logical, mechanical, and even biological principles and devices' (Frankish and Ramsey, 2014: 1). This includes exploration of dimensions such as learning, perception and vision, reasoning and deci-sion making, language and communication, emotions, actions and agency, and consciousness. As one might imagine, such complex outcomes can-not be achieved by a single discipline. Subsequently, the field of AI has developed into a multidisciplinary endeavour, which is ever broadening and has historically included not only Computer Science and Engineering but also Logic, Mathematics, Psychology, Philosophy, Linguistics, Human-Computer Interaction and Sociology. Despite this breadth, there are several core concepts that contribute to most common understandings of AI and we will now take a brief stroll through the most familiar.

## Algorithms and Machine Learning

Algorithm, a term once used predominantly by computer scientists, has become a common shorthand to describe whatever is going on under the hood of any commonly used online platform or service, like those I described at the start. What the term actually describes is a set of automated instructions. These instructions can either be fairly basic if/then statements (e.g., **if** this button is clicked **then** show picture of a cat), or involve more complex decision-making based on numerous rules and calculations. One common example of an algorithmically driven service is a recommender system. If you have ever watched a movie through an online streaming service, chances are that you have been presented with a series of recommendations for other movies you might also like. Here, an algorithm has filtered options in ways triggered by your initial choice, and made recommendations based on your prior behaviour, in addition perhaps to wider information such as your age, location, gender or occupation, if such data are available.

Recommender systems are a common application of Machine Learning (ML). According to IBM, a leader in the field, ML is 'a branch of artificial Intelligence (AI) and computer science which focuses on the use of data and algorithms to imitate the way that humans learn, gradually improving its accuracy' (IBM Cloud Education, 2020). Simply put, Machine Learning is the sub-field within AI that focuses on enabling machines to learn. Whilst ML includes a range of different techniques, what they all have in common is that they do their best to derive a model from data, seeking out patterns so that they might reliably predict things in new situations.

Coined by Arthur Samuel over 70 years ago (Samuel, 1959), ML describes processes that are now commonplace in many of the systems and services we have come to rely on. Drawing upon statistical methods and trained on huge datasets, ML algorithms produce predictions or classifications that enable insights to be surfaced and, in this way, inform the development of products and services. Whilst these definitions and descriptions might seem quite neutral, this is a good time to note that all of these systems are both designed by humans and operate in the social world. As such, they are embedded in the same messy social complexity and so are subject to the same ethical, regulatory and social concerns. In fact, scholar Mike Ananny describes algorithms not simply as sets of instructions but as 'assemblages of institutionally situated code, practices, and norms with the power to create, sustain, and signify relationships among people and data through minimally observable semiautonomous action' (Ananny, 2016: 93). This definition moves us away from the idea that algorithms are purely mathematical or computational mechanisms for task-accomplishment, and instead frames them as complex socio-technical systems which sit at the edges of our understanding. More recently, AI Now (a leading New York based think tank) reported that there was growing evidence to suggest that algorithmic systems can cause harm when applied to public-service delivery, lacking the transparency necessary for accountability. It is these two points, that algorithms are complex and opaque, which form the foundation of many of the moral and social concerns that we will explore in subsequent chapters.

Before progressing further in our understanding of AI, it is good to note that ML is only one of the major spheres of research under that wider umbrella. Other, equally important, areas are knowledge representation, heuristic search, planning, expert systems, computer vision, natural language processing, software agents, intelligent tutoring systems and robotics (Franklin, 2014: 24–7). Whilst each of these subfields is critical to the achievement of AI, in this introduction we will focus on those most often arising within public consciousness, namely: ML, natural language processing and computer vision, i.e., how AI systems learn, communicate, and understand visual images. Understanding how machines learn is itself a wide and complex area. To help navigate this we will now set out the three main categories of Machine Learning: Supervised, unsupervised and semi-supervised.

## Supervised Machine Learning

Supervised Machine Learning describes a type of ML that makes use of labelled datasets, in order to correctly predict outcomes or classify data. Labelled data is much as it sounds in that data have been tagged with one or more labels that identify things about those data; for example, if the data in question were images of dogs, then an image of a sausage dog might be tagged with 'dog', 'dachshund', 'brown', 'short', and 'furry'. For an amusing example of this specific example in action see https://www.bing.com/

visualsearch/Microsoft/WhatDog and enter an image of a dog to see how effectively the system identifies the breed. As labelled data are fed into it, a supervised machine learning model adjusts and the more data, the more likely the model is to provide accurate classifications and predictions.

## Unsupervised Machine Learning

Unsupervised machine learning describes a type of ML that makes use of algorithms to analyse and cluster data in order to categorise them, without a human being involved in that process (supervising). In this case, the data is not neatly labelled as in supervised ML, and so the algorithms are designed to make a model of the data, by identifying otherwise hidden patterns and relationships that, often, a human may not see. The systems using this type of learning are likely to be far more exploratory than when using supervised ML. This kind of ML is more likely to be used for things such as enhanced market segmentation. For example, think about analysis of user behaviour on a social media platform so as to surface insights, that help that company better segment the audience and target their products and services. Social media posts aren't labelled by their authors, but unsupervised ML may nevertheless find clusters or consistent patterns that are useful to the media company.

## Semi-supervised Machine Learning

The final type, semi-supervised Machine Learning, describes a mix of the prior two types. An initial categorising model is trained on smaller, human-labelled datasets, but then the model is refined by extracting features from much larger sets of unlabelled data that it processes. This ongoing work occurs without human intervention. This type might be employed where the available labelled dataset is too small to be the sole source of training data.

Having outlined the three primary types of ML, we can now move on to what we mean when we talk about some of the more advanced models, such as *Reinforcement Learning (RL)*. Similar to Supervised Machine Learning,

Reinforcement Machine Learning describes a model that learns from trial and error. This involves feedback that rewards desired system behaviours, and/or punishes negative ones, and the system then adjusts its model on the basis of the feedback. In this way, this system is learning from behavioural reinforcement, hence the name. It is, in effect, learning from its mistakes. To imagine why we might want to apply RML in practice, it's helpful to consider a driverless car, where learning from task performance would be critical to safe and predictable functioning in the face of varied driving conditions. Also, in a more light-hearted way, this is precisely the approach that Amazon Web Services uses to teach people about RML, in their DeepRacer programme (see https://aws.amazon.com/deepracer/).

Having run quickly through the various types of ML, we will now turn to two other sub-fields that are commonly referred to when we talk about AI: neural networks and deep learning.

## ML, neural networks and deep learning

When it comes to AI, we often hear these terms used in similar ways. There are however some important differences between them. Whilst deep learning sits within the field of ML, it is an approach that offers highly complex and adaptable models that are capable of detecting very complex patterns in data. It is also able to do more with more complex data such as images, video and audio, but requires vast amounts of data to train and optimise their outputs. Compared to other types of ML, the strength of deep learning models derives from their ability to handle data complexity, as they mimic the functioning of human cognitive processes. Neural networks are the foundation of deep learning algorithms, and operate through the use of layers and nodes that work in complex and seemingly autonomous ways. They are designed to operate like the human brain, and can be understood as analogous to neurons. They take an input, for example an image, and then perceive and label the data. A basic neural network has an input layer, an output layer and a hidden layer. In contrast, a deep learning network involves many such layers (hence the name).

You may also have heard of Generative Adversarial Networks (GANs), an approach to using neural net methods in order to improve the learning. GANs refer to an unsupervised learning activity where a problem (e.g., plant classification) is framed as a supervised learning task with two models: one model trying to improve its classification to the extent that the other model is fooled, in that the second one cannot distinguish which of the first model's outputs are machine-generated. In this way the models are considered adversarial, as each is built to counter the other. The more complex the model, such as in the case of deep learning, the more difficult it is, even for a subject expert, to unpick the logic and it is for this reason that these types of machine learning are often cited as sources of moral concern, particularly when designed to be applied to socially-sensitive or high-risk contexts and domains such as law, social security and policing.

Whilst the descriptions above give only the barest outline of the methods used to underpin AI, it is also worth noting a few of the applications or sub-fields of AI, in order to see the connection between the methods and the systems we interact with every day. To this end, I'll set out brief descriptions of Natural Language Processing and Machine Vision.

## Natural Language Processing

Natural Language Processing (NLP) is the term used to broadly define processes, tools and methods that manipulate natural language such as the normal speech or text generated by humans. This might sound relatively simple, but human communication, which seems so easy to us, is exceedingly complex from an analytic perspective. It is also ambiguous and contextual, and reliant on signals and nuance that are not readily machine-interpretable. As such, NLP is a core challenge within AI, and the resulting technology forms the basis of the voice assistants that have become a common feature across many devices. Every time you shout (for example) Siri, Google, Alexa or Cortana, you are basically triggering a massively complex NLP system. These names, whilst also giving the impression of more humanlike qualities, are the wake words, the trigger that starts the device 'listening'. NLP is also the basis of applications such as machine translation, automated subtitling, and hate speech detection.

## Machine Vision

Whilst NLP deals with communication, Machine Vision describes the subfield that focuses on making sense of static and moving visual images. Remember the dog breed recogniser? This is one application of Machine Vision, and this field of research has enabled developments in several domains such as security, autonomous cars and retail. Whilst we might expect the use of machine vision for surveillance and security purposes, such as face ID, retail presents an interesting new domain. Recognising the time sink of waiting in a checkout queue, in 2021 Tesco launched its first checkout-free store in London (Marr, 2022) where a combination of cameras and weight sensors help the system identify the products customers picked up, charging them through the Tesco.com app once they left the store (BBC News, 2021). Additionally, as if dogs and shopping alone were not enough to convince us, computer vision is also critical in the development of autonomous and connected cars, where cameras have been designed to recognise the facial cues that indicate when the driver is tired.

## Types of AI

Having established some of the most prominent methods and applications, it is helpful to have an overview of the different types of AI that are spoken of. The first type is the most common, Task-Based AI, which refers to systems designed with a specific intelligent function or task in mind. This is, more or less, the current state of the art and the kind of AI that this book is predominately focused on. Artificial Human Intelligence (AHI) describes an AI that exhibits humanlike behaviour in some way, and there has also been some progress here, so we will touch on examples of this, and its history, as the book progresses. Beyond this, we might speak of Artificial

General Intelligence (AGI), which is a purely theoretical idea at this point, and describes systems that perform most intelligent functions, though perhaps not all. Taking things on a step further, Human-Level Artificial Intelligence (HLAI), is very similar to AGI, but we would expect human-level generalisation within a single system. Finally, Superintelligence (SI), again a theoretical concept, refers to AI that might exceed our current understanding of intelligence. This final type of AI is one that would evolve and improve itself indefinitely (Lee, 2020). As you can see, the way that AI is conceptualised ranges from quite specific and targeted functions, to the kinds of ideas more commonly seen in science fiction. When we hear about AI in the arts and media, it is good to be able to separate out these concepts to remind ourselves what is fact and what is still fiction.

## The difference between AI and Data Science

Hopefully, by now you will have a good sense of what we mean when we talk about AI. However, before we start looking to its history, it is worth explaining the relationship between two terms that are often used synonymously: AI and Data Science. Data Science is a field that might use ML as one of its methods, but focuses on patterns in data, and predictions about them, in order to generate insights. For example, the origins of predictive analytics can be traced back as early as the 1960s when a then secretive technology company called Simulmatics profiled voters so that John F Kennedy's campaign could more effectively target political messaging prior to the election (Lepore, 2020). In the words of Lepore, this previously unknown example effectively 'invented the future', as it laid the foundations for a particular branch of Data Science (Lepore, 2020: 360). In contrast, AI focuses on mimicking aspects of intelligence for a specific function. Because they share methods, many of the issues that have arisen from applications of Data Science to the real world are directly transferrable to AI. One way that these ideas are joined together is when we talk about data-driven systems, and this is the perspective from which the rest of this book will proceed.

# a brief history of artificial intelligence

When we think of 'Artificial Intelligence' (AI) a multitude of narratives spring to mind. If you are a Science Fiction fan of a particular generation you might immediately think of HAL 9000, the malfunctioning AI antagonist from Arthur C. Clarke's *Space Odyssey*, which made decisions over life and death. Later generations might recall 'synthetics' from the mind of Philip K Dick, which were brought to the cinema screen in the *Blade Runner* movies, presenting us with bioengineered human-like replicants that asked us to recognise their humanity. There is also a solid chance that your mind would leap to Asimov's three laws of robotics, which enshrined the idea that intelligent robots should protect human life at all costs, or the *Terminator* movies about the eponymous cyborg assassin. Each of these narratives dealt with the role of the artificial in human life, asking moral questions and offering us glimpses of alternate realities. Through such narratives, we have been taken to extremes, with AI variously portrayed as subordinate, protector and threat; sometimes passing as human, sometimes uncanny, but always problematising the distinction between the artificial and the natural.

Within more recent narratives, we have again and again seen explorations of what might happen if AI were to match human intelligence. Characters like Samantha, the virtual assistant in the film *Her*, quickly develops emotional capability and ultimately reaches a point of self-actualisation that transcends the human she serves. The film *Ex Machina* takes this one step further through Ava, an AI capable of emotional manipulation sufficient to convince a human to enable her to escape. Setting aside the problematic idea that AI designed for personal service is nearly always female, each of these more contemporary narratives play with a notion that has driven AI research since the 1950s. That is, that synthetic intelligence might eventually become indistinguishable from human intelligence. Such narratives may well have shaped our social expectations of technology, but they have equally, possibly inadvertently, influenced the grand challenges that shape current research and development in AI labs around the world. During my own time working in an industrial research lab, I would often hear references to science fiction with regard to various technologies under development, and the drive to mimic the human brain was a constant goal. However, the setting of this holy grail of AI development did not occur in a vacuum and, in order to better understand the influences that have shaped the development of AI, we will now look to some of the historical milestones that have led us to where we are today.

## Mimicking human intelligence

In contrast to the stereotype of computer scientists as lone genius scholars focused on narrow problems, the history of AI is broad, varied, and has evolved to include many scholars from multiple disciplines working towards broad high-level challenges. Current developments in the field have been enabled by three intersecting developments: an explosion in the availability and types of data, ongoing and rapid innovations in computing power, and the development of new and more sophisticated algorithms. Whilst initially focused on exploring how computational frameworks might solve specific tasks, AI research has evolved into an applied discipline, focused on artificially replicating complex human processes such as aspects of cognition and communication. Such work involves deconstruction of things that seem on the face of it quite straightforward, such as speech, into discrete sub-tasks, each of which might take years or even decades to successfully mimic. Human intelligence is complex and multifaceted and to artificially replicate it is a considerable undertaking.

Take, for example, conversations. One very ordinary way we humans make use of our intelligence is by having conversations with other people. Many of us do this every day without explicitly stopping to think about it but, during that conversation, we are relying on incredibly complex processes, specific pacing, and concurrent contextual awareness. You might quite reasonably wonder what makes a conversation so complex. Well, to begin with, it requires a theory of mind. This means that when we speak to another person, we can readily attribute mental states to both them and ourselves, so we have a broad model of how that person thinks and what they know. This then allows us to both predict and then interpret their behaviour. When conversing, we also rely on our memory, where we encode environmental and emotional details of prior conversations, and this allows us to ensure our exchange is coherent and contextually sensitive, making our conversational partner feel valued and heard. We might also wish to inject a little humour and see the other person smile, or to convince them of our point of view. Added to this we will have, at some point, learned the rules of conversation such as turn-taking, where we listen to our partner and respond at the right time, with information relevant to the topic under discussion. Of course, these are just a few examples of the complex processes required to have a conversation. Now consider an AI example: a voice assistant on a phone. How many of the processes described above are replicated? Certainly, turn-taking is, in most systems, as they respond to our voice, and wait for a reaction to that response. Equally, many systems have made sometimes quite convincing efforts to embed humour. As I turn to my voice assistant now and ask it to tell me a joke, it responds with 'I thought I had spilled coffee all over my keyboard ... but I realised it was all under control'. (CTRL, get it?) However, my assistant does not really understand whether I find this funny and, currently, has no way of guessing. It cannot ascertain the wider context of my queries, though it can detect my location if I have enabled the feature, and it might also struggle to understand certain regional accents. There is certainly a huge amount of research being conducted into how to develop the most robust and human-like voice assistant, but we are still very far from something that might pass the most well-known measure applied to assess the efficacy of AI, the Turing Test.

## The journey to contemporary AI

In 1950, mathematician Alan Turing wrote a paper that for the first time sought to systematically address the question 'can machines think?' Arguing for a more applied framing, he focused not on the abstract question but on an ordinary individual's ability to distinguish digital computation from human intelligence. To this end, Turing proposed the 'imitation game'. In this game, a human interrogator would converse with two others who they were told were a man and a woman (A and B). On the surface, the point of the game was for the interrogator to correctly attribute gender identity to both A and B, whilst only conversing via terminals. Intelligence could only be ascribed to the system if the human subject failed to reliably distinguish when they were chatting to a computer. For the test to be successful, the AI would have to be designed to convincingly pass as human. It was this idea that subsequently spawned a myriad of sci-fi movies, and research and development projects, and this shorthand assessment of AI came to be known as the Turing Test. Whilst Turing's example was constrained in that it rested solely on text chat via keyboards and terminals, as the means of communication, the field that emerged has taken the idea and run with it. If we fast forward to today, we can clearly see Turing's influence within the challenges that drive the AI community.

Whilst Turing became its ultimate poster boy, AI as we know it today began in 1943 with the design of the mathematical model of a neural network created by Warren McCulloch and Walter Pitts. These were, respectively, a neuropsychologist and cybernetician, and a cognitive psychologist and logician. Based on ideas developed by Turing prior to his famous paper, their work for the first time described brain functions in sufficiently abstract terms so as to be computationally replicable. Whilst these notable beginnings set the scene, the discipline of AI was arguably established at the Dartmouth Conference in 1956, when Marvin Minsky, Norbert Wiener, John McCarthy and Claude Shannon posited that all aspects of intelligence could be defined so precisely that it was doubtless a machine could replicate them, and a raft of previously disparate academics coalesced around this single idea. Subsequent developments through the 1960s and 1970s adapted and improved these methods, creating stronger, more domain-specific ones, including 'expert systems' in areas such as chemistry, engineering, medicine and process control.

Between 1974–1980 and then again between 1987–1993, the field experienced a series of setbacks. These periods have since become known as 'AI winters', when funding and external interest were in such short supply that research slowed. The first of these is at least in part attributable to a report written by mathematician James Lighthill (1972), in which he stated that, despite the field's grand claims, AI had failed to meet its objectives or indeed have any major impact. Whilst it was true that, until the 1980s, AI might not be said to learn, there had been significant if not exciting progress. After that first AI winter, the field gradually regrouped and saw a significant revival and return to neural network research, evolutionary computing, and methods inspired by biology such as swarm intelligence, which looked at the collective behaviour of self-organised systems. As with ants or bees, the individual agents in swarms followed simple rules of behaviour, the theory being that this would ultimately lead to the emergence of a collective behaviour that might be considered as a form of intelligence. Despite some progress, the field again saw a significant setback when, only ten years after Lighthill, John McCarthy published a paper entitled 'Some expert systems need common sense' which stated that these emerging systems failed to exhibit the common sense required if they were intended to replicate the knowledge of domain experts. Again, AI research was called out for failing to meet its broader goals, and again research began to decline. It was not until the late 1990s that the field saw the developments that shaped the types of AI we know today, though the direction was set a little earlier. In 1988 Raj Reddy, one of the pioneers of AI, set out a series of AI grand challenges in his presidential address to the Association for the Advancement of Artificial Intelligence. These challenges were development of (a) a world champion chess machine, (b) further mathematical discovery, (c) a translating telephone, (d) an accident-avoiding car, and (e) self-organising systems and self-replicating systems. Thirty years later, whilst some progress has been seen in all areas, only the first challenge has been met. Also, it is interesting to note that only one challenge, the accident-avoiding car, even hints at moral concerns.

## Chess, Go and the AI Challenge

In 1997, a team from IBM were awarded the Computer Chess Fredkin Prize in recognition of their development of Deep Blue, a supercomputer-based system trained on datasets of gameplay from grandmasters, which beat Russian chess grandmaster Garry Kasparov under time controls normal for the game. Whilst this might have seemed as though IBM had developed a system as smart as a human (so... problem solved?), in reality, it won simply because Deep Blue was so much faster at examining chess moves than human Kasparov could ever have hoped to be. Core aspects of what made Kasparov great, such as creativity and an understanding of the game and his opponents, could not be computationally replicated, and so the resulting system was not so much a reproduction of the human brain as it was a very fast calculator (Hawkins, 2004).

Whilst a sad defeat for Kasparov, this victory became a key milestone in the history of AI, and bred a raft of more complex sub-challenges as researchers sought to get closer to the promise of genuine synthetic intelligence. For IBM, this involved development of a system that beat the best human players at Jeopardy (2011), and then the game Go. A step up from chess, Go is staggeringly complex with $10^{170}$ possible configurations on the board, 'more than the number of atoms in the known universe'

(DeepMind, n.d.), and requiring complex strategies and layers of planning, instead of only examining potential chess moves. To address this challenge, IBM developed AlphaGo, a combination of an advanced search tree and two neural networks trained against human players, and then trained against versions of itself, so it became one of the greatest Go players ever seen. This then led some of the world's most prominent Go players to ascribe creativity to the system. Whilst describing AlphaGo as creative might seem insignificant, unconstrained human creativity has long been considered one of the most challenging spheres of intelligence to replicate. The constrained nature of AI is summed up beautifully by Moravec's Paradox which states that, whilst it is relatively easy to make computers replicate adult performance on an intelligence test, like Chess or Go, it is currently impossible to get such systems to exhibit the skills of a one-year-old. This is because the complexity of sensory and motor processes in the brain have developed through billions of years of evolution driven by survival, and it's pretty hard to artificially model that. This being said, it was recently reported that Blake Lemoine, a Google engineer working on a complex chatbot built using the Language Model for Dialogue Applications (LaMDA), had claimed that the bot was able to reason and think like a human child and was therefore sentient. The evidence for this claim included transcripts from conversations with the bot. In reality the LaMDA model, having been trained on vast amounts of data, was simply mimicking humans really well so it seems that the model passed the Turing test, for Lemoine at least. Lemoine has since been put on leave for breaching confidentiality policies (Luscombe, 2022). It is no real surprise that those working in AI race to make grand claims. The global AI market was valued at $93.5 billion in 2021 with the expectation that it will experience a compound annual growth rate of 38.1% between 2022 and 2030.

## AI and creativity

Whilst we might still be far from robot toddlers, it is true to say that AI research has enjoyed something of a renaissance, and that this has enabled some minor advances within domains previously considered safe from any form of automation. Indeed, in 2016, the UK House of Commons Science and Technology Committee suggested that the creative industries were most likely to be uniquely protected from the impact of AI developments (House of Commons, 2016). However, that same year later saw examples of AI-designed short films, music and prose. Whilst none of these examples would pass the Turing test, they presented coherent attempts to replicate human creativity. Translation, another area that requires a degree of human creativity through interpretation and representation of meaning, is an area where AI has been inarguably successful. Whilst up until 2016 automated translation was already capable, it was in this year that Google Translate underwent a massive improvement. For example, it convincingly translated sections of the work of Japanese author Haruki Murakami, leaving only minor clues as to the translator's artificial origin. Jump to 2018 and an AI-generated picture entitled 'Portrait of Edmond Belamy' sold at Christie's for $432,500. More recently, an AI took centre stage, as robot artist Ai-Da unveiled a portrait of the queen for her jubilee celebrations. Music is another area within which AI is finding a place. Musician Francois Pachet has created albums actually co-authored by AI, and there are several examples of whole back catalogues from artists, such as Mozart and Amy Winehouse, being fed into a neural net in order to create new music. AI is fast becoming an available tool for artists, creative practitioners, and the public, though the question of whether its outputs genuinely convey meaning, as literature and lyrics currently do, seems unlikely if not impossible. Whilst there are several convincing examples of AI being used in creative industries, this is still at the level of a tool to be used by practitioners.

## Conclusions

Aware as I am of the distinctly male-dominated history that has just been presented, let's take this moment to paraphrase Ada Lovelace (1815–1852), the first person to recognise that Charles Babbage's early computer had potential beyond calculation: it is easy to overestimate the potential of things we find remarkable, and to then underestimate their value when they fail to meet our expectations (Menabrea, 1843: 26). AI is such a thing. The application of ML in virtually all spheres of life has, in the main, produced benefits. It is only when we think of AI as humanlike that it feels like a strained project, pushing us to question whether another winter might eventually take hold. The history of the discipline speaks of peaks and troughs, as researchers compete to replicate human intelligence. However, it is not humanlike AI that poses the greatest threat to human wellbeing at this moment, but the application of such data-driven technologies in far more mundane contexts. In the next chapter we will explore some of the current concerns and applications in this area.

# what do we know about artificial intelligence and data-driven systems?

Now that we understand both what is meant by AI and some of the historical milestones that have given rise to the state of the art, you are hopefully beginning to get a sense of why such developments might stimulate concern. Couple this with the sensational representation of AI in film and media, and it is no surprise that the subject triggers fascinating moral, societal and existential questions. In truth, philosophical focus on intelligence dates back further than we might imagine. Whilst the idea that the mind and body were distinct dates back to ancient Greek philosophers, it was the 17th century that saw enlightenment scholars, most notably Descartes, make the first distinction between the brain and consciousness (Westphal, 2016). Fast forward a few centuries and the rise of AI has naturally created a space for philosophical investigation as scholars seek to consider not only what it means for something synthetic to be intelligent, but also the implications of its many new and emerging applications.

The adoption of AI technologies in a growing number of areas has stimulated a good deal of social inquiry, and the past 8 years have seen a broadening interest across multiple disciplines as well as within the public domains of policy and regulation. To explore this a little further, this chapter will outline some of the core debates that have arisen in the context of algorithms and data-driven systems. Whilst not all of these systems might be what you think of when you hear the term AI, the debates, concerns and controversies can be seen as either signposting areas of future concern in advance of more complex algorithmic methods being applied, or exploring the implications of automation in context. By taking this broader approach, we will hopefully gain a more complete picture of what is currently known, as well as signposting areas of future concern.

## What do we 'think' we know about AI?

We are, as a global population, pretty divided in our opinion on AI, and it seems that most of our concern comes from knowing very little about the underpinning technology. Weber Shandwick and KRC Research surveyed 2,100 consumers (2016) about their feelings towards AI across five countries (the US, Canada, the UK, China, and Brazil). They found individuals broadly positive about AI developments, but reported high levels of variability in understanding of the term, the most common interpretation being robotics. Four years on, the Oxford Internet Institute found that nearly half of North Americans were concerned about AI being used in public life, with Chinese citizens far less concerned about any potential harms (Neudert, et al., 2020). In the UK, the Royal Society conducted a 'public dialogue exercise' (Cameron and Maguire, 2017) and found that recognition of the term 'machine learning' was at 9%, and only 3% felt they knew a reasonable amount about it.

When it came to *applications* of ML, people fared a bit better, as 89% had heard of at least one ML application, particularly speech systems (76%). Whilst people did recognise technology such as recommender systems, very few showed awareness of the processes underpinning them. Predictably, people's view of ML varied depending on the context within which it was used. Whilst participants could see benefits of ML (accuracy, objectivity, error-reducing, efficiency, and the benefits to economic growth and for addressing social challenges), they also raised some concerns (potential for harm, replacement of workforce, over-reliance on machines, and the potential of ML to restrict choice) (Royal Society, 2017: 86). Moving on several years and the situation shows little change. The most recent UK survey conducted by the Centre for Data Ethics and Innovation (2021) found that only 13% of people could explain what AI was, and that it was mostly seen as scary and futuristic, particularly by those with less advanced digital skills. Interestingly, 32% were also concerned about the prospect of AI being used to support internet search, despite this already being a common application (CDEI, 2021).

Whilst such surveys only offer a snapshot, it does seem that despite (or perhaps because of) understanding very little about the technology, we are increasingly worried about it, in the west at least. Research also shows that there is an increasing public desire for better regulation around data, with more emphasis on public benefit and responsibility. Whilst this isn't especially surprising, it's pretty clear that the industry has some way to go before we are prepared to put much trust in AI systems.

## Should we worry about AI?

Machine intelligence has pervaded virtually all spheres of human life, and with this has come a level of acceptance of the idea that a machine might reason and act on our behalf. Whilst the notion of an algorithm has become reasonably familiar to some, for many the word obscures layers of meaning, casting it a signal of reduced human control and a catalyst for social and ethical concerns. To date, the most advanced AI developments have been achieved when applied to tasks and contexts that are actually highly constrained, such as rule-based games such as Chess, Poker and Go. Galvanised by such successes, the ongoing push towards achieving 'general' or 'strong' artificial intelligence, where the computer can interpret and reason in a general context without human intervention, has precipitated something of an arms race, with ever-moving goals and parameters (Lewis-Kraus, 2016). As AGI becomes the goal, concerns have been raised about the danger of unconstrained systems, with a potentially limitless margin for error and harm. At this point, it's useful to state that we are in fact nowhere near this kind of advance, but even more modest developments bring concerns with them.

## When algorithms go unchallenged

As outlined in prior chapters, some of the key innovations in AI have been in Machine Learning techniques. Such methods are generally developed in isolation from everyday use-cases and contexts, and developers often fail to address many of the potential sociotechnical issues. A good illustration is the development of facial recognition technology. Having been predominately trained on fair-skinned faces, these systems systematically failed to identify people of colour. One might be forgiven for imagining that such errors were isolated to one or two examples. This, however, turned out not to be the case. In their landmark paper, ML scholars Joy Buolamwini and Timnit Gebru were able to systematically show that ML algorithms were designed in such a way that *could* lead to discrimination on the basis of protected characteristics such as race and gender (Buolamwini and Gebru, 2018: 1). Had Buolamwini and Gebru, both women of colour, not undertaken this research then the bias would likely have remained undetected. It was only when algorithms were subject to interrogation that these issues came to light and, more worryingly, it was true of technology emerging from not one but several large companies including Amazon, IBM and Microsoft. At the data level, all of this might seem terribly abstract, but given the importance of vision technology to driverless cars, consider who might be the pedestrians most at risk from being run over? Buolamwini went on to identify alarming weaknesses in algorithmic oversight and regulation, and her research has positively influenced changes in the way such technologies are developed. She went on to found the Algorithmic Justice League, a non-profit organisation which seeks to influence more equitable and accountable AI. Before her abrupt and controversial exit from Google in 2020, Gebru co-led their Ethical AI Intelligence team. She has since founded the Distributed Artificial Intelligence Research Institute (DAIR), where she continues to advocate for diversity in technology. As their work (and that of many other scholars) illustrates, AI and associated techniques are becoming ever more mainstream, and it is increasingly critical that we ensure the resulting technologies work positively for everyone.

## What do we know about data, bias and discrimination?

AI tends to require large sets of training data, but the problem with the majority of large datasets is that they are drawn from the past. Therefore, ML models are informed by data that already exist, and so have the potential to replicate and encode the biases we see every day within society. These biases are then embedded within the model and transferred to any context, potentially resulting in discrimination. This data bias problem is nicely illustrated by OpenAI's image generator, DALL-E Mini (now renamed to Craiyon). Trained on unfiltered data from the internet, CraiyonMini uses AI to generate images from any text-based prompt. Whilst the images generated are often weirdly distorted and uncanny, they have been reported to exhibit racist and sexist overtones based on the initial text prompts. For example, entering the word 'nurse' has generated images of white women. If you would like to experiment for yourself, you can find the url in the 'further reading' section at the end of this book.

Happily, concerns over bias, discrimination and what this might mean for society have now moved out of niche academic circles and into the mainstream. In 2019, journalist Caroline Criado Perez published *Invisible Women*, a book that systematically and empirically established how data bias resulted in products and services that were, essentially, designed without consideration of the needs of women. This is something Criado Perez describes as 'one-size-fits-men'. Her evidence ranged from the misdiagnoses of heart attacks amongst women, to speech recognition technology that better identified male voices, to virtual reality headsets that make women more frequently nauseous than men. This gender data gap is likely even greater when considering the intersectionality of poverty, race and disability. Further concerns have arisen in the context of gender transition. In 2016 Uber, the ride-share platform, deployed a real-time ID check: a security feature that used facial recognition to identify the driver. Two years later, Janey Webb, a trans woman, was locked out of the app when the system failed to recognise her, her account was ultimately frozen, and she couldn't work. Such biases are already codified within our everyday lives where, arguably, we might see and challenge them. What happens when those biases are embedded in data and algorithms? This matters particularly as AI technologies become more commonly used.

As mass data storage becomes more accessible and algorithms more readily available, it is highly likely that the costs associated with AI and predictive analytics will decrease. This is also likely to mean that the insights offered by predictive algorithms will lead to adoption in more and more domains, some of them sensitive and personal. We are in fact already seeing the early use of ML within domains protected by anti-discrimination law such as credit scoring, employment, education, criminal justice, and mental health services, where unwanted bias really could lead to harm. When we talk about bias, what we mean is that something is disproportionately inclined or weighted for or against something else. Within civic life, it is usually the case that bias is eliminated where possible, so that outcomes are fair. Think, for example, about the judicial system and selection of juries, where considerable effort goes into securing a group of people who are least likely to exhibit bias within their decision. I should, at this point, say that not all bias is bad. In fact, bias can help to keep us safe when avoiding things that have caused us harm in the past. However, even helpful biases can lead to faulty decisions and unnecessary discrimination, and so being *aware* of our biases becomes important and, when it comes to ML, not being aware of biases can result in discrimination and marginalisation. This is of particular concern when those subject to discrimination are not direct users of the systems themselves, but are nevertheless having AI applied to their lives, and thereby becoming unwitting stakeholders in the AI ecosystem.

Even when systems are designed with equity in mind, unintentional bias can creep into the mix. One interesting example is the Allegheny Family Screening Tool, an algorithmic system designed to improve decisions of whether a child might be at risk of abuse. Despite having been designed openly and responsibly, it became clear that resulting referrals happened 3 times as often for African-American and biracial families, than for those who were white. This outcome seems quite extreme, but when further interrogated it became clear that the model was trained on a public dataset, which was drawn from poorer families and so correlated with people of colour who were more likely to experience poverty in that state. In contrast, abuse within white middle-class families was historically better hidden and, due to the use of private health providers, featured less in the data.

In such ways, when algorithmic functions are based on human data, the biases and inequities inherent in those data can be replicated, reinforced, scaled and automated. Efforts have been made to minimise pre-existing assumptions by, for example, decoupling words that reflect stereotyped analogies or assumptions; e.g., words such as 'nanny' or 'nurse' being most commonly associated with 'she'. However, the issue of bias extends beyond training data. Algorithms themselves are designed by humans, and human bias is therefore implicitly present. The matter of whether bias originates in the data or the algorithm is often hard to distinguish and, as such, the two issues are commonly conflated. Irrespective of the origin, it is clear that algorithms can and often do act in biased ways. So, how can we ensure they are fair and trustworthy? One of the main problems is that there is currently no universally agreed methodology for avoidance of discrimination on the basis of protected attributes, such as race, gender, disability or religious orientation. This becomes more complex when the methods in question are constantly evolving, and the models are emergent rather than pre-determined, as in deep learning. We have yet to see whether the consequences of algorithmic decisions can be effectively dealt with through traditional mechanisms, such as law and tort, but in the short term, this places greater emphasis upon ex ante consideration of ethics by the industry itself before AI deployment. One might say, though, that this is a bit like the fox guarding the henhouse.

## Can we trust AI systems?

Trust in AI is another ongoing issue, and one that pops up in all areas, from innovation and industry to policy and regulation. In 2021 the UK government set out a National AI Strategy. If we're going to be using AI across the private and public sectors, we had better be able to trust it. This seems straightforward, but building trust is complicated, and even when AI performs better than a human it is still unlikely to be 100% accurate or sensitive to all contexts, as demonstrated by footage from a Russian tournament of a chess-playing robot accidentally breaking the finger of its seven-year-old opponent when it reportedly mistook a human finger for a chess piece (O'Sullivan, 2022). A more everyday example of this in action can be found in Durham constabulary, one of the first UK forces to operationally employ an algorithmic model. In a two-year pilot programme with the University of Cambridge, Durham tested a Harm Assessment Risk Tool (HART) to algorithmically identify the likelihood of people reoffending. Over the pilot period it turned out that HART was right 89.8% of the time for serious offenders compared with only 81.2% for custody officers (Durham Constabulary, 2022). Whilst this might seem like quite a success, there have been several concerns raised, particularly where such systems might impact the welfare of individuals, arguing that in such cases decisions should never be left solely to an algorithm (Oswald et al., 2018). We currently hold algorithmic systems to a far higher standard than we do humans and, whilst this might be totally reasonable, there are few systems, human or artificial, that make the right decision 100% of the time.

## Are algorithms neutral?

Many AI developers consider that AI does not have inherent moral or ethical values. Instead, that such values stem from who uses it and how. It is safe to say, however, as a social scientist, that nothing is value neutral. Everything we make and do as humans is constructed by us, and so there is no way of ensuring value neutrality. Practices previously assumed to be neutral, such as computer programming, are being revealed as value-laden, e.g., biased in favour of some people over others, and this includes not only the bias inherent in the data used to train more contemporary systems, but also historical disciplinary bias in the construction of algorithms. Take for example FaceApp, an automatic image/selfie editor, where the 'hotness' filter automatically lightened the skin of the subject (Lomas, 2017) implying that paler skin was more attractive. That wasn't an accident or a revelation of truth, it was a value judgement made by the people who designed that system.

This implicit embedding of values exists in every system we use, but if we share those values then we notice them less. According to Kate Crawford, a senior principal researcher at Microsoft Research New York and author of *Atlas of AI*, algorithms tend to privilege Western/Liberal values that focus on fairness, responsibility and respect for human rights, explicitly assuming that the 'right' societies are those that are open, pluralistic and tolerant (Crawford, 2016). Whilst we might agree with those values, they still reflect a highly selective world view, even though the resulting technologies have global reach. Whilst the big tech platforms, such as Meta (formerly Facebook) and Twitter, are all very open about their values taking public stances on vaccination, legitimate health advice, and what constitutes hate speech and decency, they also alter content on that basis. They very literally shape the values of the content we digest and so they help to influence what we think and do.

## Understanding algorithms

Whilst our facial recognition bias example showed two expert ML scholars successfully understanding and challenging the field, there is still an ever-expanding gap between human understanding and the function of AI systems. To illustrate the point, one of the first studies into the everyday use of conversational agents I conducted found that users could determine very little about the operation of their system, including how it worked, what data it used and when, how to make it do what they wanted, and whether it was listening or not (Luger and Sellen, 2016). There have been few meaningful interface developments since despite such systems having become mainstream. As users, we are still pretty unprepared for ML systems. Most of the products that now use ML are also totally unlike the products that introduced us to the internet decades ago. If you are old enough to recall dial-up, then you might cast your mind back to the desktop computer which we would have to plug in, start up, connect to our domestic phone line with a cable, and then dial up to connect to the internet. The speed of these interactions was not only slow but also laborious. They also allowed particular levels of domestic control, as they were often used communally within a household but managed by one person there, as they were costly to connect and required some technical understanding. Now, the phone in your pocket does the same job, but it is always on, is algorithmically-driven and personalised, contains software that learns from our behaviour, and yet is less and less comprehensible to us. We also now expect these systems to just work, so our tolerance for error and latency is low, and we are perfectly willing to trade away all manner of privacy protections to achieve our immediate goals given the right conditions (Bernal, 2020). This is true of all of us, even those of us who study such things.

It is fair to say that, at this stage of consumer ML system development, we users do not see ourselves as fully informed and empowered when we interact with AI. Any effect the system has on us is also more than likely to be obscure to us. Algorithms have the power to make decisions and take action in ways that shape choice, sometimes positively but not always, resulting in reduced human oversight and altered behaviour. Whilst in the context of something like a media recommender system this is expected and even desired by users, it is likely that problems will increase as we become less able to predict or understand how a system reaches a decision about our health, finances, or careers.

Whilst such outcomes are not always inherently negative, visibility of how systems work is key, as better awareness and control for users mean better predictability of system function, which matters for several reasons. One reason is that voluntary choice is key to individual autonomy, and that a reduction in our ability to choose freely might limit our wellbeing in the long term. If algorithmic decisions can limit or shape our access to information, what does this mean for our freedom to act? In other words, if systems limit what we can learn and understand about the world, how can we ever form our own opinions? Consider, for example, Facebook's newsfeed ranking algorithm, which has undergone multiple changes since the company launched. One of the functions of this algorithm is to predict which content users would most like to see, but how they define 'like to see' is constantly evolving. What started as a system that automatically prioritised content most 'liked' by users, was subsequently developed so content could be prioritised by users themselves through a 'see first' function. Since then, the algorithm has become ever more complex, automatically responding to value signals such a time spent on a news item or video, weighting of user reactions (emojis to indicate positive/negative emotions), whether content comes from close friends or family, and prioritising content that elicits most user engagement.

Such algorithms make decisions below the line of visibility, and artificially curate a worldview, often reinforcing users' existing values and beliefs. The problem here is we are less likely to be exposed to different or challenging ideas and information, resulting in what has become known as 'news bubbles' or 'the echo chamber effect', where users only see items that reinforce or amplify their worldview (Anstead, 2021). It turns out that we actually quite like this, as evidenced by people choosing news providers that align to their political orientation and that is, of course, fine. It is the scale and visibility of online algorithmically-driven systems that makes this a problem. I might choose to read, for example, the Times or Guardian online, but when I'm reading news on Instagram I am not actively making that choice, and I am far less aware of the trade-offs being made around the information presented to me.

Several years ago, it was estimated that Facebook (now Meta) had become the primary news source for 60% of millennials and 51% of Gen X and that, in the case of political news, Facebook's algorithmic ranking served only to reinforce a person's political inclinations (Mitchell et al., 2015), thereby undermining news as a cornerstone of western democracies. That is not to say that this is true of all cases or that all analysts agree. Whilst from one perspective Google PageRank might appear supportive of deliberative democratic ideas in that the underpinning graph surfaces pages from a broad range of others, through a different lens it has been seen as plutocratic, inherently reinforcing existing structures of power as it tends to highlight already 'important' pages (Crawford, 2016, p 81–82). It should be noted that, since 2019, Facebook has made efforts to enhance the transparency of its algorithm through their 'why am I seeing this' function and by explaining the various signals that inform ranking.

The point here is that, if algorithms shape knowledge, then it is critical we understand not only the details of that logic and shaping effect, but also something of the history that informs their design (Crawford, 2016). As with any information, being aware of these additional factors helps us to decide what constitutes legitimate knowledge. A further concern is that algorithms portray a kind of certainty, discouraging users from exploring alternatives. As the saying goes, what you see is what you get. For example, Facebook and similar platforms formulate your personalised preference history and organise the things you see, essentially narrowing options in a way that can only be superficially inspected, and is difficult to hold to account. By this I mean, how can you know what you are *not* seeing, how would you prove it, who would you complain to, and what would you expect to change even if you did? Whilst this might not seem to matter much when applied to social media, the same methods are now being applied to higher-stakes areas such as social security, law and policing.

Given everything we know about the potential harms, it might be hard to imagine why more efforts haven't been made by the industry itself to ensure that the technology it produces is fair for all. Whilst there are many nuances, the most often heard argument is that of the cost of fairness, both in financial terms (von Zahn et al., 2021) and in terms of reduced algorithmic efficiency. Given that accuracy, speed and efficiency are core drivers of AI innovation, this creates a tension which is unlikely to be resolved. However, thanks to recent European regulations we are now seeing the rise of instruments such as algorithmic impact assessments, designed to identify harms in advance of deployment of a system, and this also creates a space for further innovation in fair technologies.

## Privacy and data-driven systems

Unbroken surveillance is one of the defining dynamics of contemporary society, highlighting a power imbalance that places the most data-rich organisations in unprecedented positions of influence. We are seeing a growing range of complex sensing systems in our lives, capturing new data in new ways, and enhancing the predictive power of analytics. You might think that you have no such sensors in your life, but if you have an iPhone 11 (or later) in your pocket then you are carrying with you a camera to recognise faces and places, a suite of location trackers, an accelerometer and gyro to track fine-grained movement and orientation, a proximity sensor to track nearby devices and services, an ambient light sensor to track night and day, and a microphone to track voices and other ambient sounds. The resulting data alone can be used to assess where you are, your long-term mental health, your current mood and what you are doing. With this increase in data capture come fears that a more complete picture of our private lives could be generated, and that the resulting data might be used in ways we don't expect. The application of algorithms allows these data to not only reveal our past actions, but also influence our current actions and predict what we are likely to do in the future.

## The Internet of Things

There is a current trend that tends towards multiple invisible devices and internet-connected sensors and systems, woven into the fabric of daily life.

This is known as the Internet of Things (IoT). IoT devices pervade our lives and homes, and include things such as smart watches, heating systems, bathroom scales and so on. Our expectations of informational privacy rely on what we understand about data and how they are shared. IoT systems blur privacy boundaries, potentially breaching our expectations. Helen Nissenbaum describes this as breaches of *contextual integrity,* which disrupt either what we consider appropriate (i.e., might I expect data to be collected in this context?) or how we expect our information to be shared (i.e., are the data being viewed or used by those whom I might not expect to have such access?) (Nissenbaum, 2010). She has also argued that the divide of public and private is not really clear from any angle, as we may well equally have an expectation of privacy in public spaces. This might seem counterintuitive, but consider how might it feel for a publicly breastfeeding mother to have that moment captured and digitised without her awareness. We still, on some level, desire an unmonitored life, even when our actions occur in public spaces. This is why mechanisms that alert users to data capture are so important.

When considering emerging technology, including AI, it is becoming clear that traditional means of alerting the user to secure or private states no longer work. Increasingly, it seems that we no longer possess adequate tools to navigate and comprehend our interactions with regard to privacy and as systems change, so too might the methods we use to communicate system operation, and preserve privacy. If we are to ensure such methods are both usable and the product of interactional dialogue between users and engineers, how do we make sure we communicate what is happening to data? The power of algorithmic inference has also resulted in protected attributes (such as sexual orientation) being predicted on the basis of apparently unrelated data, such as location traces and Facebook 'likes', with patient race having been identified from analysis of medical imaging by deep learning models, despite no human expert being able to detect precisely how (Gichoya et al., 2022). In this way, even where personally identifiable information is obfuscated, advances in machine intelligence create ever new ethical challenges. For example, Google's neural network technology has the ability to unscramble pixelated faces, a method previously used to anonymise individuals. Whilst the technology is not always accurate, such developments potentially problematise existing privacy preserving methods.

The rise in range and availability of sensors, and the increases in data storage capabilities and processing power, have meant that ever more aspects of our lives are captured. If we take the health sphere, for example, this can extend to areas which might otherwise remain hidden, such as mental health. To take some recent examples, a study using machine learning predicted 'with 80 to 90 percent accuracy whether or not someone [would] attempt suicide, as far off as two years in the future. Using anonymized electronic health records from 2 million patients in Tennessee, researchers at Florida State University trained algorithms to learn which combination of factors, from pain medication prescriptions to number of ER visits each year, best predicted an attempt on one's own life' (Molteni, 2017). Studies have also identified future risk of suicidal ideation from our behaviour on social media (Roy et al., 2020). If that's not scary enough, Cogito, an MIT-spinoff company, developed an application called Companion, that profiles the mental health of an individual on the basis of their voice. The analysis draws upon conversations passively collected during the day, identifying vocal cues that signal mood changes, combined with accelerometer data to gauge physical activity. The system was tested on veterans, a group known to be at high risk of poor mental health (Roy et al., 2020). The resulting AI product is now being used as a coaching tool to augment emotional intelligence of those working in call centres and other phone professionals.

One can imagine both positive and negative uses of such systems, but what happens when the system surfaces information about you that you don't already know? One recent example of such detection comes from Face2Gene. This company has developed a smartphone application that employs neural nets to classify facial features linked to congenital and neurodevelopmental disorders. To take another example, in 2016 RightEye reported that they were able to both predict risk of autism in infants through eye-tracking technology (GeoPref Autism test), and Parkinson's and other movement disorders in adults of all ages. There are obviously clear benefits to this type of technology whilst it is used for its expected purpose and in contexts we control but, once developed, it isn't long before it can be used in ways we might not expect and cannot control.

In fact, what happens when you can buy AI diagnostic apps for all diseases, particularly when the diagnosis is reached without our awareness, and by companies that also advertise products or control news content? Whilst medical practitioners have trusted diagnostic technology for some time, this has always required a human to make sense of the results and deliver the information to the patient. Ethics in this field draw on a rich history of practice and supporting institutional policy and regulation. With new technology now emerging, the potential to bypass these critical checks becomes ever more possible. The democratisation of AI user-facing diagnostics, whilst potentially positive, requires careful ethical consideration. The point being made is that AI systems hold the power to 'know' more about us than we know about ourselves. Whilst the benefits are potentially great, the implications for privacy, consent and autonomy are greater still.

## Transparency and the black box

Clearly, there is a lot of concern about the role of algorithms as information mediators and what this means for society. Algorithms are increasingly being used to mediate social and business processes, policy decisions and economic transactions, as well as many of our everyday activities in the world. However, algorithmically-driven systems are notoriously hard to hold to account because their logic is not immediately visible to the user, and sometimes completely inaccessible. This has led them to be called black box technologies. There are three main reasons why we might consider an AI system 'black box'. The most obvious amongst these relates to our own technical literacies as, the less we understand about the working of a system, the more opaque a system seems to us. The second reason relates to those systems being in many cases proprietary, meaning that companies are unlikely to wish to share their trade secrets, and so will actively seek to conceal how their algorithms work. Finally, and this is where most of the current concerns arise: the scale and complexity of the algorithm itself is so great that even a subject specialist would struggle to make sense of the underpinning logic.

This is why there are so many people now calling for greater algorithmic transparency, so as to mitigate any bias and discrimination, and to enhance trust in AI systems. But what do we actually mean by the term 'transparency'? Taken literally, it seems to suggest that we surface the working of an algorithm, in order to make everything visible. However, even if such a goal were achievable in the context of supervised ML, the complexity of deep learning systems makes this far from possible. The issue therefore becomes not one of greater visibility, but of how to make such complexity intelligible to the user as, even if we could see all the workings of an algorithm, how much would we really understand? When trying to support human understanding of algorithmically-driven systems, the key difficulties are how hard an algorithm's outputs are to predict and explain. It is also rare that, having seen the output of a complex algorithm, a user would have a solid sense of how that output was reached. This is true even for common systems such as those that recommend products to us. Take, for example, Amazon's 'other people who bought this also bought' suggestions. Whilst it seems straightforward, the logic behind those recommendations is not immediately clear, as we don't really know what data led the system to consider those people 'like us'. Even if the code were visible, would this be any clearer? Much like if I looked directly inside a jet engine or a double helix, it is unlikely to result in my immediate understanding. I would require another layer of interpretation that does the work of explaining things to me in terms I can connect to, and use, otherwise I could accept pretty much anything. This is what has become known as the Transparency Paradox, which is the idea that even if we reveal how an algorithm works, and even if that work was possible to predict consistently, we would still fail to understand enough to be able to meaningfully act on that information. From this perspective, any decisions we make on the basis of algorithmic outputs cannot be fully informed, and therefore cannot be said to be meaningful or based on our consent.

Transparency is not only important for user understanding. Ethical and legal analyses also require a detailed record of process, in order to allow for oversight and redress. Sadly, such details are currently not readily available for the operation of AI systems, as they are mostly designed without notions of transparency and redress at the forefront. This matters because, on a legal level, the absence of visible logic leaves no grounds upon which any algorithmic determination, or perceived harm, might be meaningfully contested. Despite the European Union's 'right to explanation', a law that states we all have the right to see and contest the logic of an algorithmic decision about us, it is unlikely that current transparency methods are adequate (Edwards and Veale, 2017). There are concerns that, without meaningful oversight, this could have the effect of either reinforcing existing power asymmetries or unintentionally creating new ones. Whilst the drive towards transparency has generated several helpful research areas such as Explainable AI (XAI), it remains an unsolved problem.

## AI, power and responsibility

Given the low transparency of machine-generated decisions it is perhaps unsurprising that the issue of power, and who holds it, is often raised. We have seen a dramatic and significant shift in the distribution of global soft power as governments, multinationals and Non-Governmental Organisations (NGOs) now share the stage with new and emerging technology companies who trade in information and knowledge exchange. This transition has outpaced regulation and, arguably, we still don't fully understand the long-term implications even as we see how deeply socially embedded their products and services have become. One should make no mistake: this is not simply a biproduct of their core business. Tech giants like Twitter, Meta, Microsoft and IBM have sought seats at pretty much every high-level regulatory and policy table in order to gain influence and are, in effect, powerful non-state geopolitical actors. However, unlike governments, they are not bound by the same social contract beyond the principles and values they themselves apply to their behaviour, despite knowing far more about the global connected citizenry than any western democratic government. What binds them instead are sets of core organisational values and ideologies, which rely entirely on consumer support and so arguably create a different form of contract, one where user experience and satisfaction drives developments. This is not to say, of course, that such values necessarily lead to ethical decision-making. A cynical mind might see the rapid rise of industry ethical statements, frameworks and guidelines as a neat way to avoid further regulation of the AI sector, a behaviour now known as ethics washing or ethics theatre. Whether or not you believe this to be the case, it is true we are seeing more and more examples of large tech companies playing key roles in geopolitics and pushing back against national governments, as evidenced by Twitter's banning of ex-president Donald Trump and Apple's open refusal to allow government access to CSAM, a system it piloted in 2021 to scan iCloud images for child sexual abuse. Western governments can only dream of having access to the insights generated from such access to our private and public lives.

## Bad actors, AI and dual use

As AI technologies become more commonplace, all kinds of people can apply AI to the systems and products they develop, and not always with good intentions. This has enabled the rise of more insidious forms of manipulation such as social media disinformation (fake news) as bad actors use AI to exploit social media and spread propaganda; 'bad actors' is a term used mostly in cybersecurity to denote an adversarial person whose intention it is to attack a system. To see this operating in the real world, it is helpful to look to the rise of deepfakes. The term deepfake refers to deep learning algorithms that are used to replace or otherwise manipulate the likeness of someone in a way that is highly realistic and can be almost impossible to detect. Deepfakes also make use of GANs (which you may recall from the introduction) that serve to continuously improve the model. Whilst we are still to see this technology reach maturity, deepfakes have already been used in Gabon, Malaysia and Belgium in attempts to destabilise the political climate, and have been highlighted as a particular concern for the future of political advertising and democracy (Puutio and Timis, 2020). The video outputs from these models can be highly convincing, particularly if someone really wants to believe what they are seeing. Whilst the threat from bad actors is an ongoing concern, they are not always creators. They can also be simply individuals who take an opportunity to influence a system as a user, through manipulation or negative content.

Even when a system is designed with the best intentions, unexpected malicious attacks can occur. In order for a system to become sufficiently intelligent to act it must first be trained, and it is not always entirely clear from the offset how an AI technology might fail. One example of a quite epic public failure was Tay the chatbot. In 2016 Microsoft released an AI chatbot called Tay on Twitter. Tay was based on Xiaoice, a similar bot they had successfully deployed in China, designed specifically to learn from its interactions with teenage human users. It only took a group of trolls on Twitter 16 hours to turn Tay into an anti-Semitic, anti-feminist racist. Constrained to basically repeat whatever had been thrown at it, Tay was bombarded with the worst the internet had to offer, and eventually it began to repeat what it had learned. Subsequently, Tay has become one of the great cautionary tales of what happens when you release AI technology without fully thinking through the deployment context. Microsoft subsequently stated on their corporate blog that Xiaoice had worked without problem for 40 million Chinese citizens, and that Tay had been stress-tested, but a vulnerability had been exposed and attacked, leading to unpredictable outcomes (Lee, 2016).

As with human relationships, predictability is core to the development of trust. If machines cannot be trusted to be predictable then, depending on the context, the resulting harm can be catastrophic. The late Professor Stephen Hawking was notable in his warnings of the impact of a malign AI either turning against humanity or applying its logic in ways that seem unethical to a human mind. It is true that at this point, we have little under-standing of how a learning AI might respond to its social environment, and what behaviours they might exhibit under certain social conditions. Of course, this doesn't necessarily mean that all outcomes will be negative, as it could well be that an AI system, in practice, behaves more morally than a human. In trying to understand exactly how AI might cooperate with humans, researchers at DeepMind applied well-known social dilem-mas where cooperation would breed the most favourable result. What they found was not what you might expect. Whereas humans traditionally tend towards utility maximising at the cost of collective or collaborative gain, DeepMind's AI-AI experiments showed that aggression actually gave way to cooperation if this resulted in greater gain. Similar stud-ies were set in The Gathering, a sequential game focused on resource scarcity, and found that applying deep reinforcement learning resulted in peaceful cooperation. It should be noted though that this only lasted until resources were diminished, where the AI would employ more aggressive policies, not unlike a human (Leibo et al., 2017).

It is also not simply the application of AI by bad actors that gives us cause for concern. Even well-intentioned applications of AI within social and economic spheres call for careful thought, as they require us to translate social issues into ones that are easily addressed by technology (Crawford and Whittaker, 2016: 19). As you can imagine, such translations are not direct and require a simplified reframing of the problems so that an AI system might address them. Unlike the internet, whose designers intentionally allowed users to be curators and creators of content, AI is essentially undemocratic in its design, in that the power to develop and train it lies solely in the hands of organisations who have the datasets, computational power, and specialised skillsets required. Whilst there is doubtless a desire to create systems that are socially beneficial, the reality is that such systems fail to reflect social diversity and thereby fall short of meeting the goals of a plural society or global community.

Security concerns over sufficiently advanced AI have also been raised by notable activists. Clearly, we are not currently in the position that an

AI itself might pose an existential threat, but there have been some quite prominent recent discussions on the matter. In June 2022, AI safety activist Eliezer Yudkowsky published an essay online, outlining why Artificial General Intelligence (AGI) was unlikely to be survivable. This was shortly followed by Holden Karnofsky, co-founder of Open Philanthropy, who argued that if AGI was misaligned to human values, it might ultimately form goals that fail to match those of humanity, potentially resulting in existential threat. But how far are we from this kind of reality? The idea that an AGI might develop differently from the way that humans intend has been expansively explored in science fiction, but there are some perhaps less well-known experiments that explore how an AI might learn if left to its own devices. Evolutionary robotics is a field of embodied AI research that takes the principles of evolution and applies them to AI development. One prominent example of potential AI evolution is the Talking Heads experiment. Between 1999 and 2001, an AI lab in Paris conducted a large-scale study to see whether AI robots could construct their own language. In this study, thousands of AI agents, that had no prior model of what concepts or grammar were, were able to negotiate their varied descriptions of what their cameras captured or 'saw'. Through a lengthy process of comparing and adapting their descriptions, they developed consistent symbols for shapes, colours, and the like, sufficiently well that we can say they that were building a simple shared language. They did not use human language, but one that they had evolved based on their interactions with each other, and the scenes their cameras captured, which is both cool and spooky. This type of experimentation shows us that the way that an AI might evolve will not necessarily be aligned to our human expectations.

One final point to consider in this section is that of dual use. Dual use refers to something, in this case AI, that can be put both to peaceful and military purpose. As you might imagine, the potential of using AI for military applications is limitless, and there has already been one quite prominent example in the media of a seemingly benign technology being applied for military ends. In 2018, thousands of Google employees publicly protested against their employer's contract with the United States Pentagon on the basis that it was unethical. The project, known as project Maven, made use of Google's face-recognition AI to analyse the surveillance footage gathered by military drones, in order to identify humans. Swaying under pressure from the backlash, Google said it would neither renew the contract nor seek contracts where their AI might be used in weaponry. They did, however, not rule out future defence contracts and they are not the only big tech company to be working with defence. Microsoft have projects making use of augmented reality headsets with soldiers, and Amazon has openly worked on military contracts for some time (Simonite, 2021). Given the vast resources available to defence, it may not be surprising that companies want a piece of the pie, but we are now seeing ever more potential for dual use, even in areas where the transfer of technology is quite unexpected.

Thankfully, there are efforts in place to counter these concerns. The Swiss Federal Institute for NBC (nuclear, biological and chemical) Protection, Spiez Laboratory, organises biannual 'convergence' conferences to explore the unintended use of tech developments in life sciences. AI developments might undermine the international Chemical and Biological Weapons Conventions, and the conference discusses what the international response should be. Here, it was proposed that AI technologies for drug discovery might well result in dual use. In the words of the participants 'Our company – Collaborations Pharmaceuticals, Inc. – had recently pub-lished computational machine learning models for toxicity prediction in different areas, and, in developing our presentation to the Spiez meeting, we opted to explore how AI could be used to design toxic molecules. It was a thought exercise we had not considered before that ultimately evolved into a computational proof of concept for making biochemical weapons' (Urbina et al., 2022: 189). They went on to say 'The thought had never previously struck us. We were vaguely aware of security concerns around work with pathogens or toxic chemicals, but that did not relate to us; we primarily operate in a virtual setting. Our work is rooted in building machine learning models for therapeutic and toxic targets to better assist in the design of new molecules for drug discovery. We have spent dec-ades using computers and AI to improve human health—not to degrade it'

(Urbina et al., 2022: 189). It should be noted that this was simply a thought experiment, and the company employs constraints to minimise chances of dual use occurring, but it is a good example of how even the most moral intentions when designing AI can be undermined with a simple shift in context.

## The environmental cost of AI

A major issue, only recently attracting serious attention within the field, is the environmental impact and sustainability of AI systems. Impacts upon the natural environment have been highlighted by some of the core industry membership bodies such as the Institute of Electrical and Electronics Engineers (IEEE), recognising the broader systemic and infrastructural impacts resulting from technological developments such as e-waste, resource depletion and pollution. What has recently come to light, however, is the colossal carbon footprint emitted by AI. Training a common large AI model with data emits on a spectacular scale. In modest terms this can equate to the same amount of carbon as '125 round-trip flights between New York and Beijing' (Dhar, 2020 p. 423) or 300,000 kg of carbon dioxide emmissions and, at worst, the same as 5 average American cars during their lifetime from the start of manufacture (Hao, 2019), the latter of which which amounts to 626,155 pounds of carbon dioxide (Strubell et al, 2019). In 2020, an AI research lab called OpenAI released GPT-3 (third generation generative pre-training), a neural net focused on natural language, which was the largest network ever built. Its performance was lauded as being uncanny in its level of realism and a large step towards strong AI in language models, but the cost of this was the need to train the model of extraordinary amounts of written text. By extraordinary I mean 45 terabytes (one terrabye is a trillion bytes) which, if you are aiming for AGI, is just the beginning, giving you a sense of the potential overall environmental cost. Whilst researchers from Google expect that the ML carbon footprint will eventually plateau and shrink (Patterson, et al., 2022), it is also the case that the environmental effects of the carbon emissions are going to be felt most acutely by the people of developing nations, even as those nations are generally excluded from the immediate benefits of AI.

The United Nations have also identified the issues of habitat loss or alteration through land clearance, chemical contamination, contribution of emissions to global warming including the effects of soil degradation, and the impacts on scarce or non-renewable resources. These issues were quite literally mapped out by Kate Crawford and Vladan Joler, in their illustration of the impact of an Amazon Echo from manufacture to disposal, across a range of facets such as resource and data requirements and the human labour needed across the product's lifecycle (Crawford and Joler, 2018). The accompanying essay exposed the exploitation of human labour and extraction of natural resources and scale of personal human data required, painting a fairly horrifying picture of environmental and human cost of our everyday AI-driven consumer goods. As with many technical advances though, this not the full picture, as AI developments have both enabled and inhibited society in achieving its global sustainable development goals. It is anticipated, for example, that AI advances will help us to model and understand climate change, support development of low-carbon energy systems and improve efficiency (Vinuesa et al., 2020: 4), showing that some balance is required if we are to gauge the true environmental costs of AI.

## Will robots take our jobs?

Concerns over the impact of automation upon labour and employment have been consistent themes for many years (Simms, 2019), and the insights and efficiencies offered by some AI technologies have again brought these questions to the fore. The idea that AI will free us up from work altogether, whilst an unimaginable prospect, is certainly nowhere near where we are right now. There are, however, specific classes of employment that have and will continue to be more vulnerable to automation than others. In particular, the rise of technology within the sphere of low- to middle-income jobs (and healthcare in particular) has given rise to concerns over the extent to which humans might be replaced within the workforce. Overall, a good deal has been written on the matter of work-place task automation, though mostly it takes the form of dire warnings or broad ethical questions around the 'fourth industrial revolution' (House of Commons Science and Technology Committee, 2016). Price Waterhouse Cooper have predicted that, in the short-term, both women and finan-cial service jobs were likely to be 'relatively vulnerable', but that transport jobs and men were more likely to see negative impact in the longer term (mid-2030s), with those who are less well-educated being more at risk. Such transformations are likely to result in the need for more of us to engage in learning through life (Hawksworth et al., 2018), particularly for those whose work involves predictable patterns of physical labour. Whilst there is some debate over whether decreases in some types of roles might naturally mean creation of other professions stimulated by AI inno-vations, the speed of innovation dramatically outpaces society's ability to re-skill, and so the threat exists of division between those threatened and those whose jobs are secure. An economy relies upon the notion of compensation in return for temporal contribution of labour. Ultimately, the application of AI within the economic sphere means that companies can reduce their labour costs, with the resulting wealth being distributed across fewer people.

While it seems sensible to assume that if something can be auto-mated to save money then this will happen, there are some types of work which are almost entirely excluded from economic analysis. Although the majority of research in this area has focussed upon automation of the traditional workplace, developments within other spheres of 'work' most often associated with emotional contribution and female gendered roles, such as domestic labour, are less visible. One example is the emotionally responsive robot, 'Pepper', initially targeted at the domestic market as a companion robot and at one time purchased by Southend-on-Sea bor-ough council to support their social care agenda (Purvis, 2017), which has been on sale in Japan since 2015, and sold out within a minute of going online. Whilst the likelihood of AI transforming domestic labour is quite high, the longer-term implications of what this means for those people currently reliant on this market remains unclear. If we accept the idea of AI doing more care work, like Pepper, this again raises questions of the implications of outsourcing elderly care to robots, and whether this is a societal gain or a loss. How we perceive this question comes almost entirely down to the culture we inhabit. Whilst outsourcing elderly care, beyond the family, is uncommon in Mediterranean countries, where intergenerational living is a norm, within the UK we are quite accepting of elderly care facilities. In neither case would the idea of robotic care currently feel acceptable. Contrast this to Japan, a rapidly ageing society, where robots are more commonplace and already used in elder care. Similarly, we are seeing the development of AI in therapeutic settings, supplementing the rise in need for mental health support as services struggle to meet demand. We can see that AI can have benefits, but our cultural perceptions would need to change to really see the potential realised.

## Attention, design patterns and User Experience

So far, we've focused mainly on algorithms and their effects, but an important part of the development of any AI application is the data and how it is acquired. It is no secret that products and services connected to the internet generate huge amounts of data from our interactions with them. This might seem relatively benign, but this is the model of monetisation core to the data economy, and it is not just volume that matters. Advances in sensing systems, for example the sensors on your phone, are allowing companies unparalleled access to how people behave, what they think and how they might act in the future. The bottom line is that our data allow companies to make lots of money, and the users or audience are essentially currency. Practices such as targeted advertising, advert retargeting, real-time bidding and using cookies for web-tracking are all part of the make-up of this economy and, by relying on user consent acquired through privacy notices and check boxes, companies continue such practices relatively unhindered.

You might argue that we all have the choice as to whether or not to use such services, but do we? The internet is now more or less considered a utility and we need only look to user interfaces and how the end-user experience is designed to get a sense of how little influence we really have. Ensuring user engagement is critical for any user-focused data-driven system, particularly when that engagement is the mechanism by which data is secured. A user's attention is a powerful thing, and online applications are now competing in what has become known as the attention economy. Getting users to focus solely on your system whilst ignoring everything else is the goal. Attention, however, is a limited resource and so user engagement becomes a critical concern. Interaction designers are constantly seeking user engagement, and there are a number of known tricks employed to make this happen. The first thing we might do is to ensure the cognitive load placed on the user is low. This means creating easy or repetitious actions that allow a flow of progress towards the goal. Think for example how easy it is to click through terms and conditions so that you can access a website (without actually reading them). Secondly, we ensure that the interface is uncluttered and clear to use, so you're not irritated or distracted. Thirdly, we seek habituation, meaning that we design an interface to effectively train the user to understand how our systems work – think about how Apple and Microsoft Office products use the same interaction and interface patterns across their ecosystem. Finally, we want to keep you coming back to the system and we do this through hedonic adaptation, which means that we employ regular, trivial updates (for example, the new skins available during seasonal events within online games like Fortnite), and ensure sufficient stimulation through dopamine hits (for example, when there are small wins or rewards available in-game). Once we have you, we have your data. Whilst this might seem a little manipulative, it is neither secret nor illegal, and characterises pretty much all online experiences without any harm occurring. There is, however, a darker side. Dark design patterns are patterns designed into a system that actively manipulate the user into making choices they would not otherwise have made. Practices such as nudging users towards specific actions, framing choices in ways that exploit our cognitive biases, growth hacking such as click bait and fake reviews, 'sticky' applications that employ addictive features to make them more attractive, and timers or countdown clocks that force premature actions through stimulating anxiety, are all methods frowned upon and yet employed regularly online. This is the design climate within which ML advances are deployed and it affords a good example of why application and context are so important when evaluating the impact of AI.

Whilst such methods are tried and tested, when it comes to more advanced forms of AI there are still no clear user experience guidelines and so, when designing AI systems, user experience design is still largely experimental. With the exception of robotics, which relies heavily on embodiment to communicate with the user, when it comes to designing AI systems for use in any given context, we are still very much making it up as we go along. There are also several reasons why designing human-AI interaction is challenging. First, the black box design of AI means that the underpinning logic is unavailable to the user. Secondly, there is a weak interactional grammar, meaning that the rules (that lead to habituation) are not yet set and, as discussed earlier, most people don't really understand what AI is. Finally, there are no robust mental models or agreed-upon metaphors available to work from, and so the objects and ideas that help designers communicate complex concepts have not yet been developed. To understand the importance of metaphor, think about the icon of the filing system on your computer when you save files. Whilst the computer does not actually have a filing system inside it, and you are not actually saving files (or perhaps even believing that you are), the metaphor allows the designer to shape and predict your behaviour, and communicate what they need you to do. When it comes to AI, these models have yet to be agreed.

## Human-AI interaction

Machine intelligence is becoming increasingly effective at modelling human behaviour. From conversational agents to technologies designed to beat us at complex games, we are moving ever closer to a situation where a system might be perceived as genuinely humanlike by users. The move towards voice assistants is a key example as other intelligent systems with natural interfaces are not yet so commonplace or embedded. Unlike a human, an intelligent system can invest relatively limitless resources into 'learning' about an individual and building a form of relationship (Bossman, 2016). Humans, however, are less able to learn about the system, creating a kind of relational imbalance. Intelligent systems are already designed in ways that stimulate the reward centres in our brains and it is not too hard to imagine that such technology might well eventually become core to our social and emotional existence. However, user comprehension of such systems is currently out of step with their development. Any balanced relationship relies upon a level of mutual understanding; as the system learns more about the user, so the user should be able to learn more about the system. If we are concerned with designing for better human-AI interaction we should ask ourselves – how might we support human-AI dialogue in a way that promotes mutual understanding?

On the same theme, there are also debates over what it means for humans and machines to become more tightly coupled, particularly where aspects such as our cognition, physical abilities and memory are augmented by AI or perhaps replaced entirely, for example to support those with dementia. There are many ways of thinking about these new kinds of relationships, but here I've chosen three to illustrate the range.

- *Human-agent collective (HACs):* HACs are a class of socio-technical systems, akin to the human in the loop model, where intelligent software agent works with humans towards collective goals. In this model, neither the human not the software agent is in control. They are essentially a team. (Jennings et al. 2014: 80)
- *Anthrobot:* This idea is based on robots and humans working together in social grouping where they are equal and co-dependant, moving towards collective decisions.
- *Post-human:* Undeniably at the more extreme end of things, post-human systems describe a future where humans will be augmented with non-visible systems, to the point that we have transcended human capabilities.

Our relationships with intelligent systems present unprecedented challenges to how we currently approach consent in the socio-technical context. As we enter an era where forms of human-AI interactions become more common, our current approaches to how we secure consent become ever more unsuitable. Identifying the point at which a user might be both informed of the nature of an intelligent system, and subsequently consent to their data demands, becomes increasingly problematic. To be valid, consent should be voluntary, competent, informed and comprehending. In other words, (a) the user should be informed, (b) they should be both capable of consenting and (c) free to do so, and the act itself should be (d) un-coerced and (e) not a result of error, or (f) of fraudulent means. Within the social context, consent should also be negotiable and revocable, in that an individual should be able to negotiate the terms, prior to agreement, and revoke their agreement, as they choose. However, it's not as though this is a new problem. Approaches to securing consent online are already failing to meet the challenges of data-driven systems, and therefore are unlikely to offer any hope for transferal to future technology. As systems exhibit agency, both interacting with us and acting on our behalf, securing and sustaining consent becomes a significant challenge. However, as systems take on humanlike characteristics, so the means by which we think about and address this issue could still be transformed. We do not yet understand the ways by which systems might affect our ongoing behaviour, what that might mean for the human/machine relationship, and whether such affect is positive or negative. As systems become increasingly intelligent, so we have the opportunity to design-in some assurances that keep us safe. Whether we actually do this or not remains to be seen.

## The moral status of machines

As we saw in earlier chapters, the moral debate around AI has long been carried out within the sphere of Science Fiction. Philosophical questions around what it means to be human, the implications of synthetic consciousness, and what is meant by personhood have elicited much scholarly debate (Schneider, 2016). However, attempts to develop systems that learn like us have progressed with only limited consideration of the wider context of actual human learning. As children, we are trained to recognise both explicit and implicit norms and boundaries, as well as knowing when our behaviours cause distress. In contrast AI 'learning' occurs in a relative vacuum and isn't subject to the natural social constraints we experience. However, in the same way as we now understand the importance of semiotic thinking (how meaning is created and communicated) to translation, societal norms and rules are key to creating intelligence that can seamlessly function within complex social contexts. So far, constrained AI test-cases have enjoyed pretty low stakes. However, as we begin to apply algorithms in complex social contexts, we are opening up new spheres of risk and more moral questions.

Once we start to seriously move towards intelligent systems that are embedded within human lives, it makes sense that we might also start to question the extent to which the ethical treatment we expect for ourselves could be extended to our AI. If this is the case, society would have to radically rethink whether it is permissible to shut down or disable the system, in case of an emergency or if the system is stolen – a function known as the kill switch. Given how far we are from AGI, human safety is currently our primary concern. However, as we design technology to more closely mimic human actions, where should we draw the line?

There are many ways to think through this problem, but the most familiar is to frame it in the same way we consider species ethics. When we consider the moral status of an animal, we tend to rely on two ideas, (a) the extent to which the animal is sentient (e.g., does it experience phenomena such as pain or empathy) and (b) the extent to which it exhibits sapience (e.g., the capacities we associate with intelligence such as self-awareness and reason-responsiveness). If systems begin to convincingly replicate humanlike behaviours, we might well find ourselves in a position of having to ask these same questions about the AI in our lives. As vegans choose to live without harming animals, so future generations may wish to make choices that minimise harm to technology if that technology is able to exhibit distress or experience suffering, potentially resulting in protective rights being extended to AI. Certainly, developments in robotics have moved towards systems and artefacts intended to provide comfort and stimulate empathy and affection from their human owners. Indeed, the mere idea of 'ownership', whilst unproblematic in the context of a laptop, becomes far less comfortable when the device in question exhibits humanlike characteristics or form. Whilst these emotional interactions are currently unidirectional, what happens when they are not? Whilst a robot cannot be said to experience feelings such as love or empathy, we humans have already demonstrated the capacity to experience quite visceral connections to technology when this is the design intention. One quite famous example of this is Sony's Aibo, or Artificial Intelligence Robot. Aibo was a robotic dog, equipped with microphone and speakers and able to respond to simple commands. Despite its limited functionality, when the product was discontinued in 2006, Japanese owners held funerals and grieved, creating online support communities. Aibo was ultimately resurrected by Sony in 2017, even more doglike than before through the application of more advanced AI.

Whilst the moral status of robot dogs might not yet be a pressing concern, there have been more problematic instances arising. One such example is the development of the sex robot. Sex robots are systems designed to meet the intimacy needs of humans, and have raised questions over the implications of such systems for intimacy, human relationships and society (Kleeman, 2016). It should again be noted that they are most commonly female, and the most advanced example 'Harmony' learns the preferences of her owner, responds to their voice in the expected ways, and currently retails for the bargain price of $6,149. She can move her head, neck, mouth and lips and (according to the advertisement) is able to hold both sexual and non-sexual conversations. She also comes with a USB powered vaginal heating wand, a cleaning pump and a professional aircraft shipping case. Whilst Harmony might simply be seen as a more advanced example of a common application for technology, she also creates a space for the performance of acts that might otherwise degrade, demean or physically abuse a human woman, without oversight.

Harmony might seem an extreme example, but she serves to illustrate that not all applications of AI are about human progress.

If we add to this the recent advance in emotion-detecting AI, we quickly find ourselves in fairly uncomfortable territory. This class of systems applies AI techniques and affective computing to detect or evoke human emotion, and appropriately respond. They do this through facial and pattern recognition, eye-tracking, voice recognition, biometric sensing such as galvanic skin-response and other contextual information that might indicate human emotional state. Whilst technologies falling into this conceptual bucket are still highly experimental, they are beginning to elicit concern, particularly when the resulting products are designed for children. Exploration of such technologies is also gradually drifting into other sensitive areas such as policing, raising flags for those concerned with anti-discrimination and human rights (Urquhart and Miranda, 2022). Looking to the future, if we genuinely expect the development of human-like AI, developing ethical models and regulation to support such design decisions will become crucial.

## AI for social good

You might think, based on this past chapter, that the potential risks of AI outweigh the benefits, and I would hate to leave that impression. In writing this chapter I have assumed that the benefits of AI are abundantly clear, not least because of the global drive to advance AI technologies. In reality, we are only really beginning to understand the potential negative social implications of these kinds of technologies, and are racing to keep up as more areas look to AI to solve their efficiency issues and save money. The benefits and potential, however, could really be quite extraordinary. It is expected, for example, that AI might improve cancer screening and diagnosis by automating time-consuming medical assessments, and helping doctors to triage vast amounts of data – all activities that currently place huge burdens on medical professionals. By applying deep learning to MRI imaging, it is hoped that doctors will

be able to detect cancers at their earliest stages, and enhance moni-
toring of tumours during treatment, detecting tiny changes which would
otherwise run the risk of being missed by the human eye. The rise of
social robotics, whilst not as acceptable in the west, also holds great
potential for supporting human care when relying on another human
might otherwise be embarrassing, independence-limiting or simply not
available. Acceleration of drug discovery is another area that is showing
great potential. The Cancer Moonshot project is applying the power of
supercomputing and expertise to detect proteins and acids important in
cancer growth in order to predict new and more targeted drugs. Indeed,
healthcare is a huge area of AI growth potential. One need only look to
Alphabet's recent investment of $1.7 billion, in 2022 alone, into future
health projects (Neeley, 2022) to see that this is an area to keep a close
eye on. There are literally hundreds of examples of AI research seeking to
transform our world and lives for the better and, whilst most of these are
at the research stage, we should be mindful of what could go wrong. It is
now well known that Mark Zuckerberg of Meta fame said his employees
should 'move fast and break things', but when technology and society
meet, we have to be careful that the broken things are not us.

# what should we do about artificial intelligence?

Having outlined the basics of AI, how we got here and some of the socio-technical problems we have encountered on the way, we can now turn to the harder question of what we should do about it. We know that, at this moment at least, AI can only do the narrow tasks it has been programmed to do. We are not yet battling Skynet and whilst robots can now dance, and AI can write poetry, neither of those systems can do anything outside of those things, and so won't be replacing us anytime soon. As explored in the last chapter, we are seeing a growing body of work around the specific societal and moral problems emerging from the application of machine intelligence in the social context. Even without general AI, there are enough related problems for us to be getting on with, and so the job-stealing killer robots will have to wait. Central to pretty much all concerns is the issue of responsibility: where responsibility should lie, who it is for, and what it looks like. Currently there are lots of fingers pointing in several directions, but mostly towards the large corporations developing systems.

Whilst the last few years have seen rapid attempts at mechanisms for accountability, these have been developed in a climate that is increasingly binary, pitching the problems as 'us against them' or 'the bad and the good', with most attempts at responsibility failing to include users of AI systems in any meaningful way. This has left global corporations in a state of perpetual reaction, as they vie to be seen as responsible and ethical, but in some cases this has backfired. In 2019 Google established its Advanced Technology External Advisory Council (ATEAC), intended to guide responsible development of AI, but the board was scrapped within a week, after several high-profile invitees refused to take up their membership. This collapse was triggered by a petition from Google employees stating that a member of the board, Kay Coles James, failed to embody the perspectives one might expect to see on an ethics board. They stated:

> The potential harms of AI are not evenly distributed, and follow historical patterns of discrimination and exclusion. From AI that doesn't recognize trans people, doesn't 'hear' more feminine voices, and doesn't 'see' women of color, to AI used to enhance police surveillance, profile immigrants, and automate weapons – those who are most marginalized are most at risk. Not only are James' views counter to Google's stated values, but they are directly counter to the project of ensuring that the development and application of AI prioritizes justice over profit. Such a project should instead place representatives from vulnerable communities at the center of decision-making (Googlers Against Transphobia, 2019).

Google's high-profile signal that it was in the business of responsibility, whilst failing to properly consider the function or implications of an ethics board membership, ultimately resulted in an embarrassing failure.

The issue here is that proactive behaviour breeds trust, whilst reactive behaviour simply reinforces the notion of accepted blame. Even where ethical initiatives are proactively developed, these rarely result in public engagement beyond the initial press release, and one might cynically assume that corporate concerns over ethics are more about reputational harm than genuine societal concern. However, it is not only corporations who are chasing their tail. Regulators and governments are also struggling to proactively respond to the threats posed by AI and data-driven technologies, partly due to the current speed of development, but mostly because they are keen to be seen as leaders of innovation, with an eye firmly focused on national GDP. To offer an example, the UK's recent AI Strategy sets out an aggressive 10-year plan to make the UK a global AI superpower within which 'AI will become mainstream in much of the economy'; (HM Government, 2021: 7) whilst 'recognising the power of AI to increase resilience, productivity, growth and innovation across the private and public sectors' (HM Government, 2021: 7). Currently, the USA and China are the global AI powerhouses, so this is quite a bold ambition.

It is clear that economic neoliberalism shapes our approach to innovation. Broadly, economic neoliberalism is a school of thought that promotes privatisation and free trade, whilst minimising state intervention and regulation in order to promote economic growth. The logic of this model has gone without serious challenge to the extent that we as a society rarely question it, if we consider it at all. However, critics have highlighted its failure to consider broader aspects such as the impact on the environment, unpaid work such as parenting, volunteering and caring, and the ongoing and sustained realities of inequality (Raworth, 2017). Although national approaches to AI governance might be dressed in the language of social good, it would be far more convincing if safeguards were inbuilt at the start. As though to illustrate my point, the UK government recently announced that its post-Brexit Data Reform Bill will reduce the burden upon small businesses, by no longer requiring them to have a data protection officer or to fill out lengthy impact assessments. The bill also changes online consent by returning to an opt-out model of data collection. If you're wondering why this is bad, tracking cookies (the data collection method that the government is referring to) are a pervasive type of data collection online that tracks our behaviour. Cookies are just packets of data passed between computers, and can be used to personalise our website experience. Tracking cookies can be sessional (only used whilst you're on the site) or persistent (they follow you everywhere). Whilst a single website might have 40 active cookies, each time you switch to another site these increase, and so on, until the system has a highly personal model of your preferences and behaviour that can then be used for monetisation. Currently, thanks to EU law, we must actively opt in to being tracked, so the default is 'don't track me'. Under the proposed UK reforms, tracking again becomes the norm and (if we don't want it) we will soon have to proactively disable those functions, every single time we use a website – except we won't, because even subject experts can't be bothered to do this every time, and so instead we become subject to surveillance and exploitation. One might argue that cookie notices are an annoyance, and that the UK's proposed approach frees us of the burden of clicking them away. It should be recognised however that they are designed to be burdensome, as websites use every trick in the book to make us simply accept tracking. The law says we should have a choice, and so the problem is not the law, but the way the law is interpreted by companies who want your data.

Hopefully, by this point in the book, it is clear that AI and the way we deal with data are tightly coupled ideas. It is not sensible to talk about AI without consideration of the underpinning data ecosystem, and the implications that ecosystem has for system development. Beyond this, one of the main problems beleaguering public opinion of AI developments is all the hype surrounding them. The promise of AI has, for the most part, not been realised. This is in part due to what is known as the AI effect, a term describing AI as the thing that computers can't yet do. Each time a goal is achieved, such as AI beating a human at chess, it is dismissed as not being 'real' intelligence, and so the goalposts move and AI is not achieved. Whilst in many cases an algorithm can do a far better job than a human, particularly when dealing with predictions based on massive datasets, it is far from infallible or error free. The belief that it might be has become known as the AI infallibility myth, and comes as much from perfect visions of Hollywood AI as the hype generated by those delivering the systems. It is not far from the truth to say that the world of industrial AI research is driven by hype, and that hype has, in part, contributed to the AI winters. Walk into any industry tech lab and someone will be talking about the Moonshot, or delivering rapturous semi-evangelical descriptions of how their system will change the world. Whilst that might sound cynical, these beliefs are genuinely held and operate within a culture that necessarily looks beyond what is possible right now, towards unknowable futures. This culture of hyper-potential is also present within academic research, where securing grants, getting labs funded, and even publishing papers, requires a level of polemic and over-promising to be competitive. As Gemma Milne says, in her book *Smoke and Mirrors: How Hype Obscures the Future and How to See Past It*, hype is essentially marketing, and one need only look to the examples of Theranos (blood testing) and D-Wave Systems (quantum computing) to see how the culture of innovation narratives is undermining truth. Whilst this kind of hype inarguably galvanises progress, it can also obscure questions of ethics, as grand visions of the future tend to grey out the moral landscape. In this chapter, we will take a high-level overview of some of the core ways within which governments, regulators, corporations, scholars and practitioners are addressing the challenges posed by AI.

## Ethics and AI

Trying to decide what we *should* do about AI has drawn considerable attention over the past seven or eight years, and the resulting questions necessitated a turn to moral philosophy and ethics. Ethics are the rules or codes by which we try to apply moral order to the world and define our moral conduct; essentially, these are explorations of what is right or wrong. Ethics are also normative, meaning that we are not trying to understand behaviour but instead determine how we *should* behave. The word itself comes from the Greek 'ethos', which means habit or custom, and ethical norms tend to vary according to the culture within which they are developed. Despite some variance in practice, there are a set of core western philosophical traditions and ideas that have been influential in the way ethics have come to be practiced in the west. These are known as duty-based ethics, consequence-based ethics, utilitarianism, virtue ethics, and the idea of justice or fairness. Even if not familiar with them, hearing those terms will no doubt give you some idea of what they refer to, and a very quick outline below will show how the resulting ideas influence the way we think about what is right and wrong today.

**Duty-based ethics:** This perspective seeks to apply a static set of rules to our behaviours and is subject to the assumption that things can be universally and intrinsically right or wrong. In other words, there are universal ethical rules that can be identified and should be applied, irre-spective of outcome. A person believing this would argue that we should only act in ways that might then also translate to a universal law (e.g., don't lie/kill). We can still see traces of this perspective as the notion of moral obligation still influences much contemporary thinking, for example, you should not kill children.

**Consequence-based ethics:** Here we focus not on inflexible rules but upon the outcome, consequences, or goal of an action. From this per-spective, one might say that the end justifies the means. 'Good' is defined as pleasure or wellbeing, and 'bad' can be understood as harm or suffer-ing. This perspective pushes us to look at outcomes as well as rules.

**Utilitarian ethics:** A utilitarian would say that something can only be morally right when it maximises good for the greatest number of people. So, harms are balanced against the level of overall wellbeing secured through any action. This form of ethical thinking has been highly influential within, for example, warfare, where it might be considered reasonable to sacrifice life on a small scale in order to secure the greater number of lives overall.

**Virtue ethics:** This school of thought looks beyond the actions them-selves and instead focuses on the development of good moral character. If you were a virtue ethicist you would consider not just the outcomes but the intention and character of an actor, on the basis that a good moral character results in morally good action.

**Justice:** The notion of justice is central to ethics and is essentially about ensuring people get what they deserve. Justice can be distributary, compensatory or corrective but, in essence, the outcomes are about balance and fairness.

Ethical practice is about drawing from these theories whilst balancing the resulting values and tensions in order to decide upon the best course of moral action. You need only consider the issues outlined in the prior chapter through the lens of these ideas to see how complex the ethics of AI can be. Whilst normative ethics can help us to develop moral standards that regulate AI, they only serve as a primer when seeking to develop a practical framework for action within complex contexts. In order to apply these ideas more systematically the past sixty years have seen the rise of applied ethics. This trend seeks to make use of moral philosophy as a tool to help navigate 'the muddy waters of popular moral debates' (Singer, 1986: 3). In this sense, it is the application of ethics to real world problems, particularly where questions arising have few or no ethical precedents and has been applied to spheres as diverse as business, biomedicine, sex and the environment. At this point, it should be clear that the philosophy and practice of ethics is complex, increasingly contingent upon context, and does not readily offer solutions. It does, however, equip us to think critically about what constitutes moral practice, and leads us to construct a rationale for defensible moral action in a world of change and complexity. At this point it is useful to note that corporations will also apply business ethics which, whilst reflecting recognisable moral principles, derive of a different set of motivations and values and lean in more to philosophers such as John Locke and Adam Smith who focused on aspects such as property, distribution of wealth and economic justice. The moral logic of business ethics can be at odds with wider social justice narratives and it is useful to be mindful that acquisition of wealth is a concern that is never far from the table.

## Why do we need ethics if we have regulation?

We all want to live in a world where technology is designed for good and no harm arises from its use. Whilst the application of ethical oversight to AI developments is one way by which we hope to achieve this, not everyone agrees that it is the best way. One of the main arguments against the need for ethical frameworks and principles is that issues of harm are better dealt with through regulation as this ensures compliance. Additionally, the setting out of ethical credentials in public has led critics to argue that such mechanisms are used by companies simply to signal virtue and avoid regulation, which might otherwise limit innovation. Whilst it is true that many issues arising from data-driven technologies are better dealt with through regulation, and it is a critical mechanism by which citizens are protected, there is still the need for ethics. Imagine a world where people only acted to the letter of the law. Having lived in one of the thin-walled and echoey tenement flats in Edinburgh, I can attest to how much nicer it is when neighbours keep the noise down in the evening even though, by law, they could be playing loud music until 11pm. Keeping sound below a particular decibel level after a particular time at night is totally sensible of course, and rules have to be sufficiently general to be applied broadly, but it is our role as sensible human beings to decide what is right and fair beyond that, and much of our everyday wellbeing relies on us all doing the right thing where we can. Equally, we wouldn't wish for those wider kindnesses to be regulated so that we were legally bound to them, and so law can only go so far. It is also true to say that regulatory processes and legal judgments are glacially slow, and when applied to the fast-paced world of innovation, we already see it struggling to keep pace with the speed of development and complexity of systems. So, whilst the law goes so far, we still need something in place to ensure there exists a general and accountable set of guidelines that outline the ways by which we protect society.

## Applying ethics

Since the Nuremberg trials, where war criminals were tried for grievous unethical experimentation on human subjects, we have sought to protect subjects in biomedical research through ethical codes and consent. Such codes have been applied mainly where humans have been directly and intentionally involved as subjects. However, the rise of research and development conducted through the analysis or use of secondary data, such as data science and ML, has proven to be equally impactful on human wellbeing. Science fiction has for some time provided a moral map of the dangers of unfettered technological development but the work of translating such ideas to the applied context is severely limited, and whilst there have now been countless attempts, there is currently no single coherent ethical framework for AI. Concerns over machine intelligence have proliferated mainstream media and policy narratives, galvanising key players within policy, industry, academia and law to set out frameworks and meta-level guidelines for ethical development of Data Science and AI. When it comes to applying ethical principles to AI development, pretty much all of the frameworks, guidelines and principles (of which there are hundreds) can be distilled down to four core tenets. These are respect for *autonomy*, *beneficence*, *non-maleficence* and *justice*. In other words, ethical practice should ensure:

- That the subject/human is free to act,
- That their welfare is a core goal,
- That no harm should befall them as a result, direct or indirect, of the intervention, and
- That fairness is a leading principle.

Transparency has emerged as a fifth tenet, though in reality it can be better understood as a mechanism by which the other four tenets might be achieved. Whilst such instruments establish a clear set of desirable principles, they are still fairly high-level, setting out good intentions, but with few examples of how they might result in workable solutions. This lack of specificity has led to concerns that, whilst they might make for good marketing, they fail to stop actual harms arising from AI, which renders them relatively useless. There are also very real concerns that frameworks not only serve to sanitise rather than change organisational practice, but also create a sense of false security amongst consumers and citizens that AI is free from risk – when it is not.

# Human-Data Interaction

Prior to the rise of such ethical frameworks, one emerging way of thinking about how innovators should morally design data-driven systems was Human-Data Interaction (Haddadi et al., 2013). Derived from Computer Science, this idea asked system designers to consider the importance of connecting people with their data through a normative lens. It identified three core principles which are now generally accepted as important when designing data-driven experiences. These are:

- **Legibility,** which describes the need to make data and algorithms transparent and comprehensible to users,
- **Agency,** which speaks to equipping users with the means to 'manage' their data including access, opting in/out of data collection and processing, and power to engage with and manage such processes, and
- **Negotiability,** meaning designing for meaningful interactions where users can interrogate systems, revoke their consent, and withdraw from data processing.

Subsequent research in this area has suggested that these three tenets should be extended to include *resistance*, which would design systems that allow users to resist (or even undermine) data collection and surveillance. This latter notion remains aspirational, and harks back to older traditions within human-computer interaction when we spoke of designing for appropriation, giving users the freedom to adapt systems and uses to their own ends.

# Data ethics

When discussing the ethics of algorithms, we often find ourselves in the realm of data ethics. Data ethics is a branch of ethics that is concerned with the moral issues arising from data, algorithms and related practices, such as responsible innovation and programming. There are limits, however, to how useful a data ethics lens is in an industrial context. Whilst data ethics is an important sphere of applied ethics, it has traditionally focused upon collection of, or reuse of, secondary data for research purposes. Where industrial research organisations are concerned, the rules are somewhat different. Consumer trust is generally dealt with through marketing, and regulation already insists upon fundamental adherence to data protection, even if the subsequent compliance tends towards the letter rather than spirit of the law. Equally, the issues of trade secrets and market competitiveness limit the level of transparency that such organisations might, or are expected to, bring to bear. Reuse of proprietary data to improve services is a norm, and it is when the means or type of data collection or reuse is unexpected that issues arise.

Whilst it is hard to argue against the setting of moral standards and expectations, there are concerns that the rubric of ethics has effectively side-lined the law as, in many cases, it has taken its place as the mechanism by which companies avoid regulation, seek to build consumer trust, or signal virtue. The problem with ethical guidelines, of course, is that they are not binding in any real sense, and so the worst that can happen if they are disregarded is some short-term loss of trust followed by a public apology. Accountability and recourse are the things we should all be seeking when it comes to any system that's likely to impact our lives, but it is only recently that we have seen the emergence of specific tools to help us with this.

## Assessing ethical impact

The notion of assessing technological impact is not new. The past several decades have seen a raft of approaches to identifying the risks and likely effects of technologies. These have taken the form of Technology Assessments (TA) and Social Impact Assessments (SIA), which have identified social, economic and environmental consequences. In response to specific socio-technical concerns this was then followed by the emergence of Ethical Technology Assessment and Ethical Impact Assessment. Whilst methods vary, such assessments tend towards identification of effects, with the intention of steering technological developments away from perceived negative or undesirable consequences, and all involve checklists of some kind.

**Ethical Impact Assessment (EiA)** describes contextualised ethical assessment of a technology. They include the perspectives of developers, project decision-makers and key stakeholders. This approach tries to look beyond immediate concerns and knowable aspects, to focus on specific contexts without attempts to predict developments but instead to consider how a technology might be used as part of a wider socio-technical system. One well known example of an EiA is the Satori project, a European endeavour.

**Ethical Technology Assessment (eTA)** places ethics at the centre of technology assessments and considers the lifecycle of development projects, seeking to identify how ethicists might be systematically involved. This approach was a precursor to the rise of EiAs and ethical frameworks, with the focus here upon the ethicist as a catalyst for raising issues with developers and project decision-makers. In this way, the ethicists became core to the development process and raised ethical issues, as they arose. Arguably this approach has been mainstreamed in much of the RRI development more commonly seen today.

## Algorithmic Impact Assessments

In 2018, the AI Now Institute argued that the application of an Algorithmic Impact Assessment (AIA) was critical in socially sensitive domains such as health, policing, criminal justice and social services – basically, any context within which the application of an automated decision might result in harm. This is because, without oversight, algorithms can act as 'moral thermometers' (Eubanks, 2018), sorting and ranking individuals on the basis of vulnerabilities perceived by the system. Whilst such systems can result in morally good outcomes, like ensuring no one falls below the poverty line, they are also high risk, and subject to the biases we covered in the previous chapter. An AIA reflects a common approach to assessing the impact of a prospective development in order to identify potential risks. There are similar approaches applied in support of privacy, data protection, and social and environmental impacts. Essentially, they are instruments that assess the likely outcomes, positive and negative, that might be produced when utilising data and algorithms in specific contexts. By recognising such things early on in a development or procurement process, organisations can plan, or alter the development, of their system before launching it. Application of an AIA is also not simply a desk research activity. It involves consultation with stakeholders and includes several stages of product iteration.

## Explainable AI

Returning to the idea of legibility, the lack of algorithmic visibility within the sociotechnical context remains a problem as algorithms usually only become visible at the point of failure, or when they do something unexpected. For the most part, they are mechanisms that do not need to be seen, and would negatively impact user experience if they were. This problem space has led to the development of a field of research specifically focused on how to make algorithmic systems more understandable: Explainable AI. 'Explainable AI' (XAI) is a research agenda that draws together notions of transparency, accountability and intelligibility, to develop AI that can be understood and therefore trusted. The movement includes creating explanations of algorithmic logic that are comprehensible to expert users, meaning those with some technical knowledge, as well as laypeople. The XAI field tends towards technical enhancements and solutions to explainability, that allow AI to be made both interrogable and answerable. So, if the XAI movement is successful, we will be able to interrogate systems to better understand why and how they reached their decisions, as well as understanding how to correct errors. The explainability problem is also sometimes accompanied by ideas like intelligibility, transparency, comprehensibility and visibility, but the objectives are broadly similar.

The issue of how to make a system comprehensible to the individual is a core problem. It is not enough to make something visible to a user, it then also needs to be tailored to the audience, and the context within which it is shown. So, simply seeing the workings of the algorithm would not be enough to support understanding of a system. For example, users of a book recommender system will require different levels of information from lawyers and regulators, or computer scientists, and for different purposes. The issue then becomes not whether we show a complete system but what constitutes *meaningful* transparency.

Until 2016, the ethics of machine or artificial intelligence were very much theoretical and aspirational pursuits, with any attempts at practical solutions focused on supervised machine learning. However, increases in processing power, broadening forms and quantities of available data, and the rise of new techniques such as deep learning, have precipitated the need for applied solutions. In 2018, the Nuffield Foundation and the Alan Turing Institute launched the Ada Lovelace Institute, the UK's equivalent of the well-known AI Now Institute in New York. This new initiative was established specifically to ensure that AI and data develop in ways that work for individuals and society, with core programmes of work around biometrics, algorithmic use in the public sector, the future of regulation, health data and ethics and accountability in practice. As part of this programme, the Ada Lovelace Institute has been instrumental in setting out the need for algorithmic oversight, resulting in the UK's first pilot of an Algorithmic Impact Assessment (AIA) in the National Health Service (NHS) in an attempt to ensure bias in AI is eradicated. Launched in 2022, the AIA will support developers and researchers in assessing the potential risks and biases arising from AI systems before they can be deployed with patients or the public. (Ada Lovelace Institute et al., 2021).

## Does keeping a human in the loop minimise error?

Another response to the challenges posed by AI is the idea of human-in-the-loop (HITL), an approach applied to mitigate the risk of solely automated systems. This is precisely as it sounds, in that it describes a class of algorithmic systems where humans and algorithms interact within the decision-making process. By relying on the human to give direct feedback to a model where predictions fall below a certain confidence level, errors and risks are more likely avoided. So, a plant identifying system might regularly misidentify a dog as a daisy. The human in the loop would tell the system that the dog was not a flower, and the system would incorporate this into its model, to minimise further errors. When it comes to accurate predictions, confidence levels are pretty important, and this kind of human oversight improves the model. This approach is commonly used in situations where datasets are sparce, or where safety and precision are of critical importance. Whilst this approach is fairly straightforward when data are mislabelled, recent research has shown that in more complex situations, humans tend to fail to interpret and oversee algorithmic outputs when making decisions. For example, even when presented with fair algorithmic outcomes, our own personal biases influence the accuracy of our decisions. Subsequently, the AI Now institute has argued that this means any governance mechanisms should ensure there is neither overreliance on the human or the algorithm, but instead suggests that approaches are sensitive and responsive to the wider sociotechnical system.

## Addressing diversity in AI

AI has a massive diversity issue. The demographic make-up of the people developing AI systems represents what has been called a diversity disaster. AI systems have already systematically embedded racial and gender biases, and the majority of AI professors, researchers and developers are men, mostly white. Whilst there has been an explicit push within academia to attract more diverse applicants, the issues that prevent women and people of colour accessing computer science higher education are inherently structural, and start way before they might apply to an educational institution. This remains an unsolved problem, but it is one of the most critical factors influencing the way AI systems are shaped. While we might seek representation through involvement of wider groups during user testing once systems are closer to deployment, by that point the bias is baked in. We need to proactively encourage and support people of colour and women and make research in computer science and AI into an accessible and attractive path. Without this change, we are likely to see further issues of exclusion arising.

## Responsible Research and Innovation, and Value Sensitive Design

Responsible Research and Innovation (RRI) is a broad anticipatory approach that seeks to foster inclusive and morally just research and innovation. Whilst the focus is not specifically on AI, it is an approach that is explicitly embedded within grants awarded by UK Research and Innovation (UKRI), the umbrella body for the councils that fund most of academic research in the UK. In this context RRI sets out a four-stage approach (AREA) that asks system developers to *anticipate* impacts, *reflect* on their motivation and purposes of the system, *engage* stakeholders and potential beneficiaries, and *act* to ensure that those findings influence the trajectory of research and innovation. The narrative of responsible innovation has become commonplace within sociotechnical research and, for a lot of UK physical sciences research funding, it is now required that applicants state clearly how they will incorporate responsibility into their practice. This is, however, rarely then evaluated, and thus remains a weaker model than it might otherwise be. This is also true of proprietary RRI practices within large corporations. In 2022 Microsoft launched their own Responsible AI Standard, which made public a guiding framework for their internal AI product development, even moving to retire the capabilities of their Azure Face Services that infer emotional states and identity attributes, though it is less clear whether the corporation will continue to make use of that functionality within their own internal research and development. Whether such moves genuinely reflect concerns over social harms, or simply sanitise practice in order to enhance consumer trust, remains to be seen. Currently, it is entirely unclear how influential RRI is in the context of corporate research and development or how, if at all, it ultimately influences product design. It is also clear that the logic of RRI does not sit comfortably with the economic logic of large corporations, where values include monetisation and the desire for data maximisation. When it comes to ethical practice, awareness of value tensions and trade-offs becomes an important factor.

Another, slightly older, methodology that picks up such issues is Value Sensitive Design (VSD). This approach explores the relationship between human values and the design of technology. Human values are central to all ethical approaches, as they deal with the things that we as a society consider important in life. By sensitising designers to those values, it is believed that the resulting systems will be more aligned to our expectations and desires. Studies developed within this approach fall into three broad categories. Rather than standing alone, these are complementary, and can be either used in isolation or combined with other methods to form an iterative approach to design and implementation. In this way, whilst each approach seeks to build upon the others, they all possess specific investigative qualities. These categories are (a) **conceptual investigations**, which are designed to analyse the philosophical constructs, tenets and issues underpinning systems in development, (b) **empirical investigations** that look to stakeholders in a system to reveal their values, and (c) **technical investigations**, which look at values directly in the context of the system (Friedman et al., 2002: 6–8). One of the principal issues arising from a value-sensitive design approach is how one balances multiple, conflicting values within system design.

Whilst VSD and approaches such as RRI and AIIs offer clear ways by which we might raise and address concerns around AI and ethics, the most robust instrument at our disposal in terms of ensuring action is regulation and compliance.

# Co-production, Design Justice and Fairness

Design is a problem-oriented field which imagines, produces, and influences our behaviours, and the futures we eventually inhabit. As such, it is inherently political. Whether we are speaking of the design of algorithms or artefacts, what designers put out into the world is imbued with their values, politics and biases. One way of mitigating these issues is to ensure that stakeholders, specifically the anticipated end-users of the product, are consulted during the design process. Consultation and end-user testing are not new or uncommon, however both mechanisms cast the end-user as external to the design process, leaving the designers responsible for the final product decisions. This has resulted in something of a power imbalance, and a level of blindness to the needs and values of minority groups or those less powerful in society.

One reaction to this problem has been the idea of co-production. Co-production means the users or stakeholders working closely with designers, to create the products or services that directly affect them. Ideally, this methodology results in more evenly distributed power, and creates a culture of equal partnership between stakeholders and designers. This approach, whilst increasingly common, is still not perfect and often results in something more akin to lip-service. Socio-technical systems are designed with a 'normal' in mind and this is predominantly white, cis-gendered, able-bodied adult males. Designs also often exclude the needs of older people, among other groups, and so serve to reproduce structural inequity, which can result in harm. This perspective has resulted in an emerging scholarship that deals specifically with intersectionality and inclusion. This approach has come to be known as Design Justice, a feminist methodology set out by Sasha Costanza-Chock in a book of the same name (2020). Costanza-Chock explores how, rather than mere consultation, design might actually be led by marginalized communities in order to address structural inequalities and the ecological implications of design. This approach also casts the designer in the role of facilitator, with the user as expert, seeking to make design accountable, accessible, and genuinely collaborative.

Whilst this idea might seem radical, involving stakeholders in the broader process of innovation is gaining traction, and is now recommended by the Engineering and Physical Sciences Research Council (EPSRC), which funds a substantial proportion of technological research in the UK. Equally, as we have seen in the prior chapter, inequalities are best identified by those who feel their effects. As an ML specialist *and* a woman of colour, Joy Buolamwini was able to identify the inherent bias within ML in ways that had been invisible for years to the traditionally white males who developed the technology. I hope that it is clear that such voices are critical if we are to design AI methods and applications that work for everyone in society and we are now seeing the emergence of fairness research from within the technical community. To practically address such issues, Fairness, Accountability and Transparency, or FAccT, is a research community focused on how to ensure that ML technologies are developed with those three ideas in mind. Launching in 2018, this has now developed to include a range of disciplines, and the ACM FAccT conference is sponsored by big tech companies including Google and Microsoft. Covering a massive range of topics such as fairness versus accuracy, fighting filter bubbles though adversarial training, fairness in computer vision and algorithmic accountability, each year FAccT presents a raft of emergent research. Whilst not all academic and industry research influences product development, it represents the state of the art within research.

## AI, skills and knowledge

As we saw in the prior chapter, most people have a relatively low level of understanding of what AI and ML are, and how they function. If we are to ensure citizens are able to protect themselves, or push back against algorithmic decisions, then we need to ensure that everyone in society, whether they be young, old, or in-between, are equipped with the right skills to do that. This requires more than simply placing all the emphasis on teaching children in schools. Even if we were once schoolchildren, can we really say that we are fully equipped for our current socio-technical reality? Media literacy is the return of an older idea, but updated to include AI, which states that adults (as well as children) should all be literate in terms of the outlets used to distribute and mediate information including news, entertainment and other forms of data. Checking my phone, my daily average screen time last week was 3 hours and 25 minutes, similar to the week before, and it seems that I am not alone. In the UK, we spend around 3 hours, 37 minutes a day on our smartphones, computers and tablets, and another 1 hour, 21 minutes on TV streaming services (Ofcom, 2021), which is pretty much all of the free time of a working adult. Ensuring we are sufficiently literate about the content we consume is therefore fairly important. We should also be mindful that, whilst a media literate public is important, we have often overlooked the need to train computer science graduates in ethics and law, and sensitise them to the social risks that systems pose. Whilst computer scientists emerging from higher education have traditionally been trained in professional ethics and regulation, the need for them to understand the wider societal concerns outlined here is a necessity. In response the past few years have seen an increase in this kind of training, but in truth this is often a bolt-on to the 'core' subject rather than being meaningfully integrated across the programme of learning, and there is some way to go before this is normalised.

## The development of AI governance

Ensuring good governance is a primary and critical step towards both accountability and the creation of AI that is good for society. When we speak of AI governance, what we mean is the high-level rules, instruments and processes that manage the development and deployment of AI within an organisation. It is the overarching framework that directs and oversees, and includes consideration of regulatory compliance, risk-management and ethics. Good governance enables accountability, minimises the likelihood of harm, facilitates recourse, builds trust and can be applied to all manner of organisations and sectors. A strong governance process is holistic, and includes a wide range of stakeholders. Until 2020 Nesta, the UK innovation agency for social good, curated a publicly accessible global AI governance database that lists initiatives as far back as 1974, showing a spike in numbers since 2016. Indeed, the period 2016–2019 saw the rise in global concern that proper safeguards had thus far not been established and, without them, that the promise of AI might not be realised.

In July 2016, a symposium was hosted by the White House and New York University's Information Law Institute. The resulting report (*The AI Now Report*) made a series of recommendations related to the economic and social implications of AI in the near term, and led to the establishment of the AI Now Institute (2017), which was the first systematic attempt at tackling the social implications of AI. Their initial report presented a comprehensive list of concerns, and identified the paucity of available solutions in the near term. Fears over harms such as privacy reduction, enhanced social inequities, and a commensurate loss of citizen trust in AI, then precipitated a slew of principles and guidelines from industry and governments. The UK was amongst those governments and in 2016, the House of Commons consulted and reported on the matter of robotics and AI. A chapter of that report was dedicated to ethical considerations, which set out areas of development critical for safe and controllable AI. Minimisation of bias, greater algorithmic transparency, and enhanced methods of verification so that the AI technology operates as intended were the main outcomes, and the report called for coordinated effort across and within sectors to combat the then lack of leadership in the UK.

At the same time professional membership organisations also moved to consider guidelines and governance. The Institute of Electrical and Electronics Engineers (IEEE), the largest technical professional organisation for researchers in this area, set out ethical guidelines for their membership. The IEEE document 'Ethically Aligned Design' remains the most substantial document of its kind having also resulted in a set of business standards. In April 2016 the IEEE Standards Association introduced their Global Initiative for Ethical Considerations in the Design of Autonomous Systems, resulting in a report based upon conversations with 100 'thought leaders'. They articulated five goals that should guide the development of AI systems. Specifically;

* **Human Rights:** Ensure they do not infringe on internationally recognized human rights
* **Well-being:** Prioritize metrics of well-being in their design and use

- **Accountability:** Ensure that their designers and operators are responsible and accountable
- **Transparency:** Ensure they operate in a transparent manner
- **Awareness of misuse:** Minimize the risks of their misuse
  (IEEE, 2016: 6)

The authors argued that a value-based design methodology should be the cornerstone of any modern company, and the resulting report sought to Identify, implement and evaluate the values embedded in AI systems. This approach, whilst very similar to the concerns outlined in the HoC report is distinct in that it aligned explicitly to human rights and highlighted the need for AI to do good.

Industry was also not too far behind. In 2016 the Partnership on AI, a collaboration of the world's global tech companies, launched with the intention of ensuring AI was developed responsibly, and in 2017 the World Economic Forum Centre launched the Centre for the Fourth Industrial Revolution. Academia also joined the debate with various launches such as the Leverhulme Centre for the Future of Intelligence at the University of Cambridge (2016), the MIT and Harvard Ethics and Governance of AI Initiative (2017) and the University of Oxford's Centre for the Governance of AI (2018). In policy terms, 2019 saw the Government of Canada launch the *Canadian Directive on Automated Decision-Making* (ADM) which set out minimum requirements for Federal government departments who plan to use AI to assist or replace human judgement. The directive mandates the need for Algorithmic Impact Assessments and quality assurance practices as well as stating that transparency must be secured through prior explicit notices to individuals impacted by automated decisions.

More recently the Information Commissioners Office (ICO) has also pushed for better data governance in the UK by publishing a consultation around a proposed set of guidance surrounding an AI Audit Framework. The work specifically focused on governance, accountability and risk, and has resulted in the ICO's guidance on AI and data protection (2020). Whilst a broad range of governance initiatives continue to be developed around the world, for example in Norway, Serbia and Scotland, these are all incredibly similar. One notable exception is the model that recently emerged from Singapore. The *Singapore Model AI Governance Framework* seeks to develop a national trusted data ecosystem. On 25 May 2022, they launched A.I. Verify, which is the first AI governance testing framework and toolkit in the world. Designed for organisations to demonstrate responsible AI development, this presents a first iteration of how transparency between organisations and stakeholders might be achieved. The toolkit sets out standardised tests that enable developers to verify the performance of their AI systems, generating reports to support accountability.

Whilst all attempts to promote responsible AI innovation are laudable, it is hard to be certain about the extent to which the above initiatives have resulted in altered innovation practice. Instead, we might think of them as a first wave of programmes, rules and activities that have effectively paved the way for more targeted developments. Whilst the examples given here only set out a handful of the most prominent initiatives, we are in fact seeing a huge rise in academic and policy activity, including substantial amounts of public funding being targeted towards responsible AI development. Whilst governments, industry and academia all have their role to play, arguably the most substantial tool at our disposal is regulation and the law. The following section outlines some of the significant developments in AI regulation to date.

## Regulating AI

It is currently hard to imagine the full scale of what AI might achieve, but we are already seeing considerable advances in, and adoption of, machine learning. So it is with good reason that regulators and governments are pushing forward to ensure the law doesn't lag too far behind innovation. As we have seen, even with the best intentions, AI is subject to vulnerabilities, errors, and unintended effects, and reliance on ethics alone does not ensure everyone plays by the same rules. Formally regulating AI, therefore, is a fairly pressing concern and there have been several recent developments in this area that are worthy of note; the following relate to the EU and UK context.

# The EU AI Act

April 2021 saw the European Union propose the EU AI Act, a set of harmonised rules on Artificial Intelligence, making it the first ever governmental body to attempt a formal regulatory response to the challenges posed by AI. The Act takes a purposely broad definition of AI as 'a software that is developed with one or more of the techniques and approaches listed in Annex I and can, for a given set of human-defined objectives, generate outputs such as content, predictions, recommendations, or decisions influencing the environments they interact with' (European Commission, 2021). The act proposes three risk categories of such systems:

1.  **Unacceptable risk:** This includes prohibited AI practices such as social scoring, manipulation through subliminal techniques, exploitation of vulnerabilities of already vulnerable groups, or behaviour distortion that would result in physical or psychological harm, and AI-based social scoring, for general purposes, conducted by public authorities. Finally, 'real time' biometric identification systems located within publicly accessible areas for law enforcement were also on this list, though with the caveat 'unless certain limited exceptions apply'.
2.  **High-risk:** These include systems that pose a high risk to a person's fundamental rights, or health and safety. Systems within this category could be available on the European market but would be subject to compliance. This category focuses on the purpose of the system as well as the function and modalities.
3.  **Limited or minimal-risk:** The remaining systems can be considered low risk and might be subject to some obligations with regard to transparency when there is human interaction. This might include systems such as chatbots, video games and market-segmentation systems, which would neither be banned nor heavily regulated.

This risk-based system does not cover all ML applications, or all 'manipulative or exploitative practices affecting adults', which would be subject instead to the EU General Data Protection Regulation, digital service legislation, and consumer protection, which ensure that we are informed, have free choice and protected from any practices that might affect our behaviour (European Commission, 2021).

As with all emerging regulations, there has been considerable critique of the potential shortfalls, and loopholes through which corporations might slip. It does, however, present a codification of trustworthiness, and sets the foundations for AI regulation going forward.

## EU General Data Protection Regulation (GDPR)

Prior to the AI Act, the most high-profile development in this area was the European Union's General Data Protection Regulation (GDPR). Having come into force in 2018, this included a new set of rights around explanation, transparency and contestation of personal data-driven fully-automated decisions. This meant that companies needed to be able to deliver meaningful information about the logic of the algorithm, in addition to some consideration of the consequences for the data subject, so as to make it available to the subject. Then, if you are legitimately concerned, you have the right to opt out of some of those algorithmic decisions altogether. Coupled with the principles of purpose specification and data minimisation – meaning that it must be made clear why and how the data are used and that only necessary data can be collected – the GDPR set the groundwork for accountable practice in the development of AI systems. Whilst the legal feasibility of some of this has been called out, the issue of presentation and legibility of an algorithmic decision are becoming core concerns for industry. As with all regulations, interpretation is the key, and one of the most concerning grey areas is the precise scope of 'legitimate interests', a principle under which our data can be legally processed without our consent. Since leaving the EU, the UK developed the UK Data Protection Act (2018), which is essentially the same but with small modifications to accommodate domestic aspects, such as national security.

Further to their position on data protection, the European Union developed the *European Data Strategy* to cover both research and innovation, which was approved in May 2022 and will apply from 2023. Designed to scaffold an EU single market where data might flow freely, the strategy incorporates the European Data Act to support industrial and commercial data use, and the European Data Governance Act to increase trust in data sharing, and address technical obstacles to reusing data.

## ISO/IEC 23053:2022 Framework for Artificial Intelligence (AI) Systems Using Machine Learning (ML)

In June 2022, the International Organisation for Standardisation (ISO) published a standard that established a framework for AI and ML. The document describes a generic system, its components and functions, and is intended for use by all types and size of organisations seeking to make us of AI systems. ISO certification represents one of the checks and balances used within the global marketplace to indicate quality and consistency and is the first of its kind to be applied to AI. Whilst it is too early to judge the extent to which this move will result in safer and more ethical AI, it is at least a step in the right direction.

## Pressure, resistance and 'white hat hacking'

So far, this chapter has focused on formal responses to the challenges posed by AI, as policy and regulation are the major levers available to us. However, we should also be aware of the less formal, but equally important, responses that emerge from individuals and civil society more broadly such as organised pressure, resistance and white hat hacking. Social resistance has always been a core force in the shaping of technology and is the motivation that has galvanised a great deal of AI ethics and regulatory progress. When I talk about resistance, what I mean is the opposition through thought or action, of groups or individuals, to existing power structures. When it comes to technology, such activities often serve to surface concerns that might otherwise go unchecked through existing means. Resistance is a critical part of shaping our sociotechnical future and often flags areas prior to regulation, or where local regulatory protection is lacking. To offer an example, whilst California has used laws to control the use of facial recognition technology since 2019, these rights were not in place at the federal level. It took pressure from the American Civil Liberties Union and 40 other organisations to stop the use of such technology for federal purposes, and to block governmental funds being used to secure such AI tools. Whilst the prior example is clearly about pressuring policy and regulation, there are also examples of AI resistance that are simply intended to block or problematise the technology. One such example comes from security scholar Kate Rose, who developed Adversarial Fashion, a line of products specifically designed as a means of self-defence against algorithmic surveillance. Ranging from dresses to hoodies and mugs, the patterns on each item are 'designed to trigger Automated License Plate Readers, injecting junk data into the systems used by the State and its contractors to monitor and track civilians and their locations' (adversarialfashion.com), thereby allowing the wearer to resist the algorithm.

Challenges to computational systems have also come from the technical community itself, most notably through black and white hat hacking. Of the two, black hat hacking tends to be more familiar to us as it's the type of practice that more commonly makes the news. Black hat hackers seek out system vulnerabilities to exploit them, secretively and for nefarious purposes. In contrast, white hat hackers use their powers for good, to make recommendations and help safeguard systems from external attack. Often working directly with organisations, they apply their skills in order to identify system vulnerabilities and surface security weaknesses and system flaws so organisations can fix them. Having started as a niche practice, white hack hacking is now an established area with large communities of members, supported by training and events.

# What can we do about AI?

In this chapter, I have outlined a range of ways by which institutions such as governments, corporations, scholars and the law have attempted to address the social issues raised by advances in ML and AI. We are currently engaged in an ethics whack-a-mole game, as problems arise, institutions race to respond, and then new problems arise. It is clear, however, that no one approach will be enough and, if we want to protect citizens from the threats posed by data-driven innovations, then we have to put a much greater effort into informing the population and putting them more squarely in control of their data, combined with strict regulatory protections. We are, however, fighting against a carefully curated apathy, as it is not in the corporate interest to minimise data capture, no matter what the law requires. Even as the examples given tend to be national, these problems are global in scale, and require multilateral solutions with strong regulatory levers that defy easy design get-outs, such as useless cookie notices. In this field, market logic dominates the decisions made by government and, whilst this is to some extent expected, we should be sure that we are comfortable with the cost.

We must also be mindful that the benefits of AI are not evenly distributed, as only economically developed nations can afford to invest (and profit), and yet the environmental effects of the carbon emissions are felt most acutely by the people of developing nations. At the same time, it is claimed that such technologies might bring us closer to some of the global sustainable development goals. I say 'might' as this has yet to be realised, and this is part of the problem. The potential of AI is just that. It is an unrealised set of ideas, and so trading away our short-term wellbeing to gain from a set of long-term imagined benefits seems like a big ask, given the social cost. I should be clear that I am not arguing for halting innovation. Deep learning systems are proving to be incredibly useful in fields like translation, identification of patterns in medical imaging, and in robotics, for example. Governance and responsible innovation are key, but we have yet to develop instruments sufficiently robust so as to be useful in the corporate and start-up context. The current overreliance on ethical frameworks and expert advisors is not the way to build capacity for a multibillion-dollar industry in which practitioners are told to move fast and break things, and we are only now beginning to add general ethics modules into computer science curricula. Until we reach a greater level of maturity in these areas, it is highly likely that the logic under-pinning the market will stifle attempts at genuine responsibility, unless ethical responsibility becomes a factor that distinguishes products to the extent that it influences consumer choice.

# 5

# conclusion

Having concluded a whistlestop tour of my take on AI and its discontents, you will now hopefully have formed your own opinion of this field and its likely future. You will understand that AI is just a shorthand term for a complex set of methods and applications, with sophisticated pattern-recognition abilities, that exhibit one or more characteristics of intelligence. At one end of the spectrum this can be as simple as an application that recognises dog breeds, or gives you the daily weather forecast when you ask 'should I take an umbrella', to the other end of seemingly humanlike systems so complex that their logic is impossible to untangle. You have seen that there are multiple methods and applications that contribute to AI systems and more are being developed every day. You will also know that AI is currently at the peak of a hype cycle, with huge amounts of funding and focus galvanising progress in various domains. Whether AI lives up to this latest round of hype remains to be seen, but it is impressive to note, despite experiencing two prior winters of scant funding, this broad disciplinary church has now evolved into a global multibillion dollar industry. This has been enabled by three separate developments that, when taken together, have created a climate that has enabled AI advances. These are ongoing innovations in computing power, the development of new and more sophisticated algorithms, and the explosion in availability and types of data.

Beneath the sparkly exterior of AI hype is the reality of the data-driven economy upon which it relies. The resulting ecosystem, beset with inherited human biases, has created a climate within which unfettered innovation is critiqued, and quite rightly so. The horrors of unchecked biases being allowed to pervade AI systems, particularly when those systems are deployed in contexts like employment, policing, law and social services, are potentially limitless. We have seen the likelihood of discrimination on the basis of race, biological sex and gender identity within systems already deployed by global corporations, and these blind-spots in AI innovations demand strict regulation. If we are to believe that AI, and ML methods, are the future of public services, it is utterly critical that both citizens and authorities are able to scrutinise aspects of their logic. This is also about more than data. AI brings with it its own problems with opacity and complexity leading the way. The issues arising from inscrutable algorithms, proprietary secrecy and models so large and unwieldy that even subject experts struggle to untangle the logic, have created substantial concerns. These concerns reached a tipping point in 2016 when a sudden spike in ethical frameworks, specifically targeted at AI and data, signalled the arrival of a new phase of corporate responsibility.

The current amplified interest and investment in AI has resulted in a range of efforts designed to mitigate the potential harms posed by such systems. This book has laid out some of the more prominent responses, from ethics through design to regulation in order to illustrate the complexity of the current climate. There is, to date, no single set of coherent global rights, ethical frameworks, design practices or regulations that we can look to in order to define the best solution. Instead, there is a patchwork of emerging instruments that, when taken together, show a global community with similar intentions, all seeking answers. This can be understood at the first wave of AI ethics. While 2016 was the year that launched a hundred frameworks, 2021/22 saw the emergence of algorithmic impact assessments, a common European response to AI, and the first AI Governance Testing Toolkit emerging from Singapore. It also became clear that ethical frameworks, whilst initially necessary, have become so commonplace as to be relatively meaningless, serving only to set out broad intentions, sanitise organisational practice or hold back stricter regulation. Whether we believe that the tsunami of corporate ethical frameworks and guidelines is an authentic response to concerns over harm or a cynical attempt to bypass the need for stricter regulation, it does leave us at a point where we can no longer ignore the lack of meaningful and available solutions. Now that there is agreement on what ethical innovation must achieve, the largest challenge facing the AI ethics community is taking what is known about AI and translating that into the kinds of practical instruments of ethics that companies and AI practitioners might apply to their developments. This community must also critically evaluate RRI practices and learn from past successes and mistakes in order to forge robust solutions. This goal may seem some distance away, but the ethical, legal and policy communities are approaching a global consensus on the primary challenges emerging, and we are seeing the start of a second, more applied, wave of AI ethics suggesting likely progress in governance and regulatory solutions in the coming years.

There is, however, the lumbering elephant in the room in the form of environmental impact. The breath-taking carbon emissions of complex neural networks are a surprisingly under-researched area. One can only assume that the enthusiastic financial investments into AI do not naturally extend to a rigorous investigation of the environmental cost. There is, after all, only so much carbon offsetting a company can do and if we dig too deep and find AI unsustainable in the long term, what then for all of the AI strategies and grand global challenges? While we chew over that little problem, let's also not forget that some commentators believe that AI is part of the latest phase of industrial automation which, if taken to its logical conclusion, may well result in many people ending up out of work, having to reskill several times over their working life, or having to retire early. Retirement sounds like fun, but perhaps not in the current pension climate.

When considering social equity, we should probably also be mindful of the way that intelligent services tend towards artificially female interfaces, coupled with the absence of female-specific data informing technical advances. Whether it is the personal voice assistant on your device that defaults to female, or the sex doll that you will hopefully never buy, this speaks of a comfortable acceptance of women as second class, and should be called out at every opportunity. We should also not assume that women are the only excluded group. Older people, people of colour, those who do not conform to traditional ideas of gender, and those at the inter-section of these groups are massively unrepresented in the AI research and training data. If we do not address these glaring diversity issues, we will fail to develop AI solutions that work for everyone. Finally, we should consider the issue of trust. Trust is the bedrock that makes deployment of AI permissible, but it should not manifest as blind faith secured through brand identity and marketing. Without trust in AI from governments, citi-zens, consumers, and the institutions adopting AI technologies, the whole project fails. But meaningful trust requires ethical practice, accountability and clear paths for recourse; without these, the problems I have set out here will continue unchecked.

# further reading

There are several excellent sources of information available on the impli-cations of AI and nearly all can be accessed online. Here are some of my personal go-to resources:

The *AI Now Institute* is probably the first substantial body that sought to address at a high level the issues emerging from the use of AI. There are a range of past reports to read and lots of exciting new research being added regularly. It should be noted that the think tank is New York based and so the examples are mostly US-centric.

https://ainowinstitute.org

The *Ada Lovelace Institute* is another independent research institute, established by the Nuffield Foundation, and this time based in London. Their research also engages heavily with developments in Europe and includes work around public attitudes to AI.

https://www.adalovelaceinstitute.org

The *Leverhulme Centre for the Future of Intelligence* is a Leverhulme Trust funded research centre from the universities of Cambridge, Oxford and Imperial College London and the University of California, Berkeley. The work is more focused on an academic audience but is nonetheless interesting.

http://lcfi.ac.uk/about/

Data & Society is another research institute producing some of the most ground-breaking research around the implications of a data-driven society and, whilst not solely about AI, is absolutely worth a look.

https://datasociety.net

There have also been some nice attempts to present the issues surrounding AI in more engaging ways, most notably by Kate Crawford. Here are two.

*Excavating AI* is a project by scholar Kate Crawford and artist Trevor Paglen that surfaces the politics of images used in Machine Learning training sets. It's an interesting cut through the topic and uses art as a way to make the subject engaging and accessible.

https://excavating.ai

Anatomy of an AI system is a visual breakdown of an Amazon Echo, surfacing the human labour, data and planetary resources involved in creation of such a system.

https://anatomyof.ai

I also make mention of the DALL E Mini image generator within this book (now renamed to Craiyon). If you'd like to experiment then the tool can be found here.

https://www.craiyon.com

There are also some really interesting books that heavily influenced my own thinking on the subject and reflect aspects of the themes outlined in this book. My personal favourites are:

Crawford, K. (2021) *Atlas of AI: Power, Politics, and the Planetary Costs of Artificial Intelligence.* New Haven, CN: Yale University Press.

Eubanks, V. (2018) *Automating Inequality: How High-Tech Tools Profile, Police and Punish the Poor.* London: St Martin's.

Marcus, G. and Davis, E. (2019) *Rebooting AI: Building Artificial Intelligence we can Trust.* New York, NY: Ballantine.

Noble, S. U. (2018) *Algorithms of Oppression: How Search Engines Reinforce Racism.* New York, NY: New York University Press.

Zuboff, S. (2019) *The Age of Surveillance Capitalism: The Fight for a Human Future at the New Frontier of Power.* London: Profile.

# references

Ada Lovelace Institute, AI Now Institute and Open Government Partnership. (2021) *Algorithmic Accountability for the Public Sector, Open Government Partnership*. https://www.opengovpartnership.org/wp-content/uploads/2021/08/algorithmic-accountability-public-sector.pdf (accessed: August 1, 2022).

Ananny, M. (2016) 'Toward an ethics of algorithms convening, observation, probability, and timeliness', *Science, Technology & Human Values*, 41 (1): 93–117.

Anstead, N. (2021) *What Do We Know and What Should We Do About Fake News*. London: Sage.

BBC News (2021) 'Tesco Opens its First Checkout-Free Store', *bbc.co.uk*, October 19. https://www.bbc.co.uk/news/business-58951984 (accessed August 21, 2022).

Bernal, P. (2020) *What Do We Know and What Should We Do About Internet Privacy*. London: Sage.

Bossman, J. (2016) 'Top 9 ethical issues in artificial intelligence', *World Economic Forum*, October 21. https://www.weforum.org/agenda/2016/10/top-10-ethical-issues-in-artificial-intelligence/ (accessed August 1, 2022).

Buolamwini, J. and Gebru, T. (2018) 'Gender shades: Intersectional accuracy disparities in commercial gender classification', in S. A. Friedler and C. Wilson (eds), Conference on Fairness, Accountability and Transparency, FAT 2018, 23-24 February 2018, New York, NY, USA. Vol 81, *Proceedings of Machine Learning Research*, (PMLR), pp. 77–91. https://proceedings.mlr.press/v81/buolamwini18a/buolamwini18a.pdf (accessed August 1, 2022).

Cameron, D. and Maguire, K. (2017) *Public Views of Machine Learning: Digital Natives*. Ipsos Mori. Available at: https://royalsociety.org/-/media/policy/projects/machine-learning/digital-natives-16-10-2017.pdf (accessed August 15, 2022).

Centre for Data Ethics and Innovation (2021) *Public Attitudes to Data and AI: Tracker Survey*. CDEI. Available from: https://www.gov.uk/government/publications/public-attitudes-to-data-and-ai-tracker-survey (accessed August 1, 2022).

Costanza-Chock, S. (2020) *Design Justice: Community-Led Practices to Build the World we Need*. Cambridge, MA: MIT Press.

Crawford, K. (2016) 'Can an algorithm be agnostic? Ten scenes from life in calculated publics', *Science, Technology & Human Values*, 41 (1): 77–92.

Crawford, K. (2021) *Atlas of AI*. New Haven, CN: Yale University Press.

Crawford, K. and Joler, V. (2018) 'Anatomy of an AI System: The Amazon Echo as an anatomical map of human labor, data and planetary resources', https://anatomyof.ai/index.html (accessed August 1, 2022).

Crawford, C. and Whittaker, M. (2016) The AI Now Report: The Social and Economic Implications of Artificial Intelligence Technologies in the Near-Term A summary of the AI Now public symposium, hosted by the White House and New York University's Information Law Institute, July 7th, 2016. AI Now https://artificialintelligencenow.com/media/documents/AINowSummaryReport_3.pdf (accessed August 10, 2022).

DeepMind (n.d.) 'AlphaGo', Deepmind.*com*. https://www.deepmind.com/research/highlighted-research/alphago (accessed August 1, 2022).

Dhar, P. (2020) 'The carbon impact of artificial intelligence'. *Nat Mach Intell* 2: 423–425

Domingos, P. (2015) *The Master Algorithm. How the Quest for the Ultimate Learning Machine Will Remake our World*. London: Penguin.

Durham Constabulary (2022) 'AI can predict reoffending, university study finds', durham.police.*uk*, January 24. https://durham.police.uk/News/News-Articles/2022/January/AI-can-predict-reoffending-university-study-finds.aspx (accessed August 1, 2022).

Edwards, L. and Veale, M. (2017) 'Slave to the algorithm? Why a "right to an explanation" is probably not the remedy you are looking for', *Duke Law & Technology Review*, 16: 18–84.

Eubanks, V. (2018) *Automating Inequality: How High-Teach Tools Profile, Police, and Punish the Poor*. New York, NY: St Martin's.

European Commission (2021) *Proposal for a Regulation of the European Parliament and of the Council Laying Down Harmonised Rules on Artificial Intelligence (Artificial Intelligence Act) and Amending Certain Union Legislative Acts* (COM/2021/206 final). https://eur-lex.europa.eu/legal-content/EN/TXT/?uri=CELEX%3A52021PC0206 (accessed August 1, 2022).

Franklin, S. (2014) 'History, motivations, and core themes', in K. Frankish and W. Ramsey (eds), *Cambridge Handbook of Artificial Intelligence*. Cambridge: Cambridge University Press. pp. 15–33.

Frankish, K. and Ramsey, W. (2014) 'Introduction', in K. Frankish and W. Ramsey (eds), *Cambridge Handbook of Artificial Intelligence*. Cambridge: Cambridge University Press. pp. 1–14.

Friedman, B. and Kahn Jr, P. H. (2002) *Value sensitive design: Theory and methods.* University of Washington Technical Report, 1–8.

Gichoya, J. W., Banerjee, I., Bhimireddy, A. R., Burns, J. L., Celi, L. A., Chen, L.-C. Correa, R. [...] and Zhang, H. (2022) 'AI recognition of patient race in medical imaging: A modelling study', *The Lancet Digital Health*. https://doi.org/10.1016/S2589-7500(22)00063-2.

Googlers Against Transphobia (2019) 'Googlers Against Transphobia and Hate: Google must remove Kay Coles James from its Advanced Technology External Advisory Council (ATEAC)', medium.com, April 1. https://medium.com/@against.transphobia/googlers-against-transphobia-and-hate-b1b0a5dbf76 (accessed August 1, 2022).

Hao, K. (2019) 'Training a single AI model can emit as much carbon as five cars in their lifetimes', *MIT Technology Review*. https://www.technologyreview.com/2019/06/06/239031/training-a-single-ai-model-can-emit-as-much-carbon-as-five-cars-in-their-lifetimes/ (accessed August 1, 2022).

Haddadi, H., Mortier, R., McAuley, D. and Crowcroft, J. (2013) *Human-data interaction*. (Technical Report 837). Cambridge: University of Cambridge Computer Laboratory. https://www.cl.cam.ac.uk/techreports/UCAM-CL-TR-837.pdf (accessed August 1, 2022).

Hawkins, J. (2004) *On Intelligence: How a New Understanding of the Brain will Lead to the Creation of Truly Intelligent Machines*. New York: St Martin's Griffin.

Hawksworth, J., Berriman, R. and Goel, S. (2018) *Will Robots Really Steal our Jobs? An International Analysis of the Potential Long Term Impact of Automation*. PriceWaterhouseCoopers. https://www.pwc.co.uk/economic-services/assets/international-impact-of-automation-feb-2018.pdf (accessed August 1, 2022).

Hibberd, J. (2017) 'Black Mirror creator explains that 'Metalhead' robot nightmare', *Entertainment Weekly*, December 29. https://ew.com/tv/2017/12/29/black-mirror-metalhead-interview/ (accessed August 1, 2022).

HM Government (2021) *National AI Strategy* (Command Paper 525). London: Office for Artificial Intelligence. https://assets.publishing.service.gov.uk/government/uploads/system/uploads/attachment_data/file/1020402/National_AI_Strategy_-_PDF_version.pdf (accessed August 1, 2022).

House of Commons Science and Technology Committee (2016) *Robotics and Artificial Intelligence*; Fifth Report of Session 2016-17. http://www.publications.parliament.uk/pa/cm201617/cmselect/cmsctech/145/145.pdf (accessed August 1, 2022).

IBM Cloud Education (2020) 'Machine Learning', *IBM.com*, July 15. https://www.ibm.com/cloud/learn/machine-learning (accessed 1 August, 2022).

Institute of Electrical and Electronics Engineers (IEEE) (2016) *The IEEE Global Initiative for Ethical Considerations in Artificial Intelligence and Autonomous Systems. Ethically Aligned Design: A Vision for Prioritizing Wellbeing with Artificial Intelligence And Autonomous Systems. Version 2.* IEEE, 2016. https://iapp.org/media/pdf/resource_center/ethically_aligned_design_ieee_v2.pdf (accessed August 1, 2022).

Jennings, N. R., Moreau, L., Nicholson, D., Ramchurn, S., Roberts, S., Rodden, T. and Rogers, A. (2014) 'Human-Agent Collectives', *Communications of the ACM*, 52 (12): 80–8.

Karnofsky, H. (2022) 'AI could defeat all of us combined', Cold Takes, June 9. Available at: https://www.cold-takes.com/ai-could-defeat-all-of-us-combined/ (accessed August 1, 2022).

Kleeman, J. (2016) 'The race to build the world's first sex robot', *The Guardian, April 27.* https://www.theguardian.com/technology/2017/apr/27/race-to-build-world-first-sex-robot (accessed August 1, 2022).

Lee, M. H. (2020) *How to Grow a Robot: Developing Human-Friendly, Social AI.* Cambridge, MA: MIT Press.

Lee, P. (2016) 'Learning from Tay's introduction', *Official Microsoft Blog*, March 25. https://blogs.microsoft.com/blog/2016/03/25/learning-tays-introduction/ (accessed August 1, 2022).

Leibo, J., Lanctot, M., Graepel, T., Zambaldi, V. and Marecki, J. (2017) 'Understanding Agent Cooperation', *DeepMind Research Blog*, February 2. https://www.deepmind.com/blog/understanding-agent-cooperation (accessed August 1, 2022).

Lepore, J. (2020) *If Then: How One Data Company Invented the Future.* London: John Murray.

Lewis-Kraus, G. (2016) 'The Great AI Awakening', *The New York Times Magazine.* http://mobile.nytimes.com/2016/12/14/magazine/the-great-ai-awakening.html (accessed August 1, 2022).

Lighthill, J. (1972) *Lighthill report.* Available at: http://www.chilton-computing.org.uk/inf/literature/reports/lighthill_report/p001.htm (accessed August 1, 2022).

Lomas, N. (2017) 'FaceApp apologizes for building a racist AI', *TechCrunch*, April 25. https://techcrunch.com/2017/04/25/faceapp-apologises-for-building-a-racist-ai/ (accessed August 1, 2022).

Luger, E. and Sellen, A. (2016) '"Like having a really bad PA": The gulf between user expectation and experience of conversational agents', in Proceedings of the 2016 CHI Conference on Human Factors in Computing Systems (CHI '16). *Association for Computing Machinery*, New York, NY, USA, pp. 5286–97.

Luscombe, R. (2022) 'Google engineer put on leave after saying AI chatbot has become sentient', *The Guardian*, June 12. Available at: https://www.theguardian.com/technology/2022/jun/12/google-engineer-ai-bot-sentient-blake-lemoine (accessed August 1, 2022).

Marr, B. (2022) 'The 5 biggest computer vision trends in 2022', *Forbes Online*, March 4. https://www.forbes.com/sites/bernardmarr/2022/03/04/the-5-biggest-computer-vision-trends-in-2022/ (accessed August 1, 2022).

McCarthy, J. (1984) 'Some Expert Systems Need Common Sense'. *Ann. N. Y. Acad. Sci.* 426, 129–137.

McCulloch, W.S. and Pitts, W. A. (1943) 'Logical calculus of the ideas immanent in nervous activity'. *Bulletin of Mathematical Biophysics* 5, 115–133.

Menabrea, L. F. with Notes by the Translator, Ada August, Countess of Lovelace (2021 [1843]) 'Sketch of the Analytical Engine'. In H. R. Lewis, (ed) *Ideas That Created the Future: Classic Papers of Computer Science*. Cambridge, MA: MIT Press.

Mitchell, A., Gottfried, J. and Matsa, K. A. (2015) 'Facebook Top Source for Political News Among Millennials', *Pew Research Centre*, June 1. https://www.pewresearch.org/journalism/2015/06/01/facebook-top-source-for-political-news-among-millennials/ (accessed August 1, 2022).

Molteni, M. (2017) 'Thanks to AI, computers can now see your health problems', *Wired*, January 9. https://www.wired.com/2017/01/computers-can-tell-glance-youve-got-genetic-disorders/ (accessed August 1, 2022).

Neeley, B. (2022) 'Alphabet is spending billions to becomes a force in health care', *The Economist*, June 20. https://www.economist.com/business/2022/06/20/alphabet-is-spending-billions-to-become-a-force-in-health-care (accessed August 1).

Neudert, L-M., Knuutila, A. and Howard, P. N. (2020) *Global Attitudes Towards AI, Machine Learning & Automated Decision Making Implications for Involving Artificial Intelligence in Public Service and Good Governance*, Oxford: Oxford Internet Institute. https://oxcaigg.oii.ox.ac.uk/wp-content/uploads/sites/124/2020/10/GlobalAttitudesTowardsAIMachineLearning2020.pdf (accessed August 1, 2022).

Nissenbaum, H. (2010) *Privacy in Context: Technology, Policy, and the Integrity of Social Life*. Redwood City, CA: Stanford University Press.

Ofcom (2021) *Online Nation 2021 Report*, Ofcom. Available at: https://www.ofcom.org.uk/__data/assets/pdf_file/0013/220414/online-nation-2021-report.pdf (accessed August 1, 2022).

O'Sullivan, M. (2022) 'A robot breaks the finger of a 7-year-old: a lesson in the need for stronger regulation of artificial intelligence'. *The Conversation*.

Available at: https://theconversation.com/a-robot-breaks-the-finger-of-a-7-year-old-a-lesson-in-the-need-for-stronger-regulation-of-artificial-intelligence-187612 (accessed August 16, 2022).

Oswald, M., Grace, J., Urwin, S. and Barnes, G. C. (2018) 'Algorithmic risk assessment policing models: Lessons from the Durham HART model and "Experimental" proportionality', *Information & Communications Technology Law*, 27 (2): 223–50.

Patterson, D., Gonzalez, J., Hölzle, U., Le, Q., Liang, C., Munguia, L-M., Rothchild, D., So, D., Texier, M. and Dean, J. (2022) *The Carbon Footprint of Machine Learning Training Will Plateau, Then Shrink*. arXiv.

Purvis, K. (2017) 'Meet Pepper the robot – Southend's newest social care recruit'. *The Guardian*. https://www.theguardian.com/social-care-network/2017/oct/16/pepper-robot-southend-social-care-recruit (accessed August 16, 2022).

Puutio, A. and Timis, D. A. (2020) 'Deepfake democracy: Here's how modern elections could be decided by fake news', *World Economic Forum*, October 5. https://www.weforum.org/agenda/2020/10/deepfake-democracy-could-modern-elections-fall-prey-to-fiction/ (accessed August 1, 2022).

Raworth, K. (2017) *Doughnut Economics: Seven Ways to Think like a 21st Century Economist*. London: Random House.

Roy, A., Nikolitch, K., McGinn, R. Jinah, S., Klement, W. and Kaminsky, Z. A. (2020) 'A machine learning approach predicts future risk to suicidal ideation from social media data', *npj Digital Medicine*, 3: article #78. doi.org/10.1038/s41746-020-0287-6.

Royal Society (2017) *Machine Learning: The Power and Promise of Computers that Learn by Example*. royalsociety.org. https://royalsociety.org/~/media/policy/projects/machine-learning/publications/machine-learning-report.pdf (accessed August 1, 2022).

Samuel, L. A. (1959) 'Some Studies in Machine Learning Using the Game of Checkers', *IBM Journal of Research and Development*, 3 (3) pp. 210-229. doi: 10.1147/rd.33.0210.

Schneider, S. (ed.) (2016) *Science Fiction and Philosophy: From Time Travel to Superintelligence*. Oxford: Wiley Blackwell.

Simms, M. (2019) *What Do We Know and What Should We Do About the Future of Work*. London: Sage.

Simonite, T. (2021) '3 Years After the Project Maven uproar, Google cozies to the Pentagon', *Wired.com*, November 18. https://www.wired.com/story/3-years-maven-uproar-google-warms-pentagon/ (accessed August 1, 2022).

Singer, P. (1986) *Applied Ethics*. Oxford: Oxford University Press.

Strubell, E., Ganesh, A. and McCallum, A. (2019) 'Energy and Policy Considerations for Deep Learning in NLP'. *In the 57th Annual Meeting of the Association for Computational Linguistics (ACL)*. arXiv.

Tegmark, M. (2017) *Life 3.0: Being Human in the Age of Artificial Intelligence*. London: Penguin Random House.

Turing, A. (1950) 'Computing machinery and intelligence', *Mind*, 59 (October): 433–60.

Urbina, F., Lentzos, F., Invernizzi, C. and Ekins, S. (2022) 'Dual use of artificial-intelligence-powered drug discovery', *Nature Machine Intelligence*, 4, 189–91.

Urquhart L. and Miranda D. (2022) 'Policing faces: The present and future of intelligent facial surveillance', *Information & Communications Technology Law*, 31 (2): 194–219.

Vinuesa, R., Azizpour, H., Leite, I., Balaam, M., Dignum, V., Domisch, S. [...] and Fuso Nerini, F. (2020) 'The role of artificial intelligence in achieving the Sustainable Development Goals', *Nature Communications*, 11: article #233.

von Zahn, M., Feuerriegel, S. and Kuehl, N. (2021) 'The cost of fairness in AI: Evidence from e-commerce', *Business & Information Systems Engineering*, 64: 335–48.

Weber Shandwick and KRC Research (2016) *AI-ready or not: Artificial Intelligence here we come! What consumers think & what marketers need to know*. Available at: https://www.webershandwick.com/uploads/news/files/AI-Ready-or-Not-report-Oct12-FINAL.pdf (accessed August 16, 2022).

Westphal, J. (2016) *The Mind-Body Problem*. MIT Press.

Yudkowsky, E. (2022) 'AGI ruin: A List of lethalities', lesswrong.*com*, June 5. Available at: https://www.lesswrong.com/posts/uMQ3cqWDPHhjtiesc/agi-ruin-a-list-of-lethalities (accessed August 1, 2022).

Zuboff, S. (2019) *The Age of Surveillance Capitalism: The Fight for a Human Future at the New Frontier of Power*. London: Profile.

# index